1

MDT

**DATE DUE**

W9-ADL-888

**Deat**

GAYLORD

PRINTED IN U.S.A.

# Death in a Promised Land

*The Tulsa Race Riot of 1921*

**Scott Ellsworth**

Foreword by John Hope Franklin

Louisiana State University Press

Baton Rouge and London

Copyright © 1982 by Louisiana State University Press
All rights reserved
Manufactured in the United States of America

Designer: Albert Crochet
Typeface: VIP Trump Medieval
Typesetter: G & S Typesetters, Inc.


Library of Congress Cataloging in Publication Data

Ellsworth, Scott.
    Death in a promised land.

    Bibliography: p.
    Includes index.
    1. Tulsa (Okla.)—Riot, 1921.    2. Tulsa (Okla.)—Race
Relations.    I. Title.    II. Title: Tulsa race riot of 1921.
F704.T92E44                976.6'86                81-6017
ISBN 0-8071-1767-6 (paper)                AACR2

Louisiana Paperback Edition, 1992
01  00  99  98  97  96  95  94  93        5  4  3

AAW-9977

*To my mother and father*

That which we do is what we are. That which we remember is, more often than not, that which we would have liked to have been; or that which we hope to be. Thus our memory and our identity are ever at odds.

—Ralph Ellison
"The Golden Age/Time Past"
(1959)

# Contents

# Illustrations ⸻

# Foreword

In the spring of 1921 I was only six years old, but the events in Tulsa in late May and early June were permanently etched in my mind. For some years my family had been living in Rentiesville, an all-Negro village some sixty-five miles south of Tulsa. I was born there, in the post office, where my father was postmaster, the justice of the peace, president of the Rentiesville Trading Company, and the town's only lawyer. There was not a decent living in all those activities; and when my father left in February, 1921, to open a law office in Tulsa, the family was to follow in the summer. As my mother completed her teaching stint in Rentiesville that spring, I was as anxious as my brother and sister (our older sister was away in a Tennessee boarding school) to move to the big city.

Then it happened! Tulsa was burning! The news of the Tulsa riot reached the little village slowly and piecemeal. In 1921 there were no radios or television sets, of course. And Rentiesville had no telephones, or even a telegraph to connect it with the outside world. We had to depend on news of the riot that was relayed from Tulsa to Muskogee, where it was printed in the *Daily Phoenix*, which was dropped off at Rentiesville by the Katy Railroad mail and passenger train. Black Tulsa had been destroyed, burned out, we learned. Many blacks had been killed. But the paper did not say who they were, and we had no word from my father. Our mother put the best interpretation on the news, trying to allay our fears. It seemed like years before we learned a few days later that my father was safe.

In 1921 and for the next few years, the significance of the Tulsa riot to me was that it kept our family separated. The assets that my father had accumulated in those few months in Tulsa were destroyed in the riot, and our move there had to be postponed indefinitely. Meanwhile, my father was busy fighting city ordinances that seemed designed to obstruct black Tulsa's efforts to rebuild. In that he was successful, but success in bringing the family together again came more slowly. His clients were poor people, and it took time to collect the small fees they could afford. Finally, on Thursday, December 10, 1925, my mother, who had quit her teaching job, packed our belongings and moved to the home in Tulsa that my father had rented for us.

Everyone who experienced the race riot in Tulsa or was touched by it in some way, as I was, had his own view of what happened, what was the aftermath, and what were the long-range consequences. When I arrived in Tulsa, at ten years of age, the collective wisdom in the black community had made certain conclusions about the riot. One was that Dick Rowland, whose allegedly improper advances toward a white girl precipitated the riot and who was later acquitted, was, along with all the black Tulsans, the victim of "riot fever" raging in the white community. Another was that many more whites were killed during the riot than any whites were willing to admit. If one went to court regularly, as I did with my father in the late twenties, one would be interested to hear cases involving the estate of some white person who died on or about June 1, 1921. One was always tempted to conclude that the deceased lost his life in the riot. Another view was that whites looted the homes of Negroes before burning them. Rumor had it that following the riot, Negro women would encounter white women wearing clothing or carrying some item recognized by the Negro women, who would simply claim the property and take it.

These conclusions seemed necessary for the continued self-esteem of Tulsa's black community. Whether or not the conclusions were valid, they had the desired effect. The self-confidence of Tulsa's Negroes soared, their businesses prospered, their institutions flour-

ished, and they simply had no fear of whites. After 1921, an alterca-
tion in Tulsa between a white person and a black person was not a
*racial* incident, even if there was a loss of life. It was just an incident. Such an attitude had a great deal to do with eradicating the fear
that a Negro boy growing up in Tulsa might have felt in the years
following the riot.

Scott Ellsworth has done a magnificent job both of researching the
riot and writing about it. Sixty years have passed, and there are not
many people alive who are able to recall the events with the relia-
bility that the historian requires. One must be extremely careful,
moreover, in using sources, oral or written, about an incident involving such deep emotions. Ellsworth has written with care and
good judgment, appreciating the full dimensions of the tragedy, but
resisting the temptation to be pretentiously maudlin or excessively
moral. We all have our personal versions of the riot, but Ellsworth
has written an account of the events that comes as close to being *the*
definitive history of the Tulsa riot as I have seen. In doing so he has
written a version for all of us, meanwhile warning us to be careful in
the way we use our own version. On his behalf I invite the reader
to take most seriously his account, which has both integrity and
authenticity.

John Hope Franklin

**Death in a Promised Land**

Prelude

# In the
# Promised Land

I

Bill Williams once asked his father why he had come to Oklahoma. "Well," he replied, "I came out to the promised land." Indeed, when John Williams and his wife Loula came to Tulsa during the first years of the twentieth century, it was for them a place of promise. John was from Mississippi; Loula was a Tennessean. John had worked for a railroad in his home state, and his knowledge of steam engines helped him to secure a job in Tulsa at the Thompson Ice Cream Company, which used steam power to make its products. Although John and Loula Williams were by no means the first black residents of Tulsa, they came at a time when the city's black and white populations, though growing, were still relatively small. There was not a black doctor in Tulsa, then located in Indian Territory, in 1905 when Loula gave birth to Bill. She chose to travel to Hot Springs, Arkansas, to a black physician there.

John's work at the ice cream company paid well enough that the Williamses became the first black Tulsans to own a car. In those days, most automobile owners would repair their own cars, and John was very adept at working on his. As Tulsa's population climbed and more and more Tulsans purchased automobiles, many of them took their cars to John Williams for repair work. This extra source of income soon became so lucrative that John quit work at the ice cream company and opened a full-time garage of his own, along Greenwood Avenue, which soon became the center of the city's black business district.

About 1912, the Williamses built a three-story brick building on the northwest corner of Greenwood and Archer avenues. On the first floor was a confectionary, complete with a twelve-foot fountain and table seating for nearly fifty people. If John had a mechanical mind, Loula had an entrepreneurial one, and the confectionary which she managed soon became a money maker. She sold ice cream, candy, and sodas, and this confectionary was one of black Tulsa's first commercial refreshment spots other than bootleg whiskey joints. On the second floor of the building was the apartment where the Williams family lived, while the third floor was rented out as office space to dentists, doctors, and lawyers. Greenwood, as the district was called, was fast growing into a thriving business center.

Then, in 1914, John wanted a bigger garage for his growing automobile business, so the Williamses erected another building, a two-story brick structure, further up Greenwood Avenue. The second

John, Loula, and Bill Williams, about 1912. Their automobile is a 1911 Norwalk.

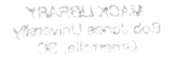

story was a twenty-one-room boarding house, and the first floor was to be John's new garage. John soon found out, however, that there was a city ordinance against having a rooming house above a garage, so he decided to keep working at his old one. John and Loula were then faced with what to do with the empty first floor. The answer came when they read in a newspaper that a theater in Oklahoma City had gone bankrupt, so they purchased its equipment and created the Williams Dreamland Theatre, the first black theater in Tulsa. Silent movies, accompanied by a piano player, were shown and live entertainment was scheduled as well. Loula, assuredly the managerial family member, ran the theater.

In the best American entrepreneurial tradition, the Williams family prospered.

## II

On May 31, 1921, sixteen-year-old Bill Williams, together with some of his classmates at the Booker T. Washington High School, was busy decorating a rented hall on Archer Street for the senior prom which was to be held that night. Other students were rehearsing for the graduation exercises not far away on Greenwood Avenue. But before young Williams and his classmates could finish their decorating, an adult came in and told them to go home. They were told that it looked like there might be some racial trouble that evening. Having read that afternoon's Tulsa *Tribune*, which carried the headline TO LYNCH NEGRO TONIGHT,[1] Bill had already sensed this. But rather than go directly home, he headed for the Dreamland Theatre, where his mother was at work. Inside the theater, a man got up on stage and told the audience, "We're not going to let this happen. We're going to go downtown and stop this lynching. Close this place down."

Shortly thereafter, around eight or nine o'clock in the evening, black Tulsans began to gather on Greenwood near Archer, in the heart of their business district. Some of the men had guns. Soon, groups of men drove downtown in cars, and John Williams was one of those who went. Bill wanted to go, too, "to see what was going on," but his mother would not let him. Instead, the two of them went home, to their apartment above the confectionary. John came

The Dreamland Theatre.
Courtesy of W. D. Williams

Bill Williams, top left, *ca.* 1921.
Courtesy of W. D. Williams

home about midnight, after the shooting had begun, and told the family—Loula, Bill, and a young man named Hosea who stayed with them—to go to bed.

Loula had been remodeling the family's apartment shortly before that night, and she had an inside wall removed near the back of the apartment, leaving only the exposed plumbing and ventilation pipes. When Bill Williams woke up the next morning, around five or six, he found his father in the back, resting his 30-30 rifle against the exposed pipes. A repeating shotgun was also at his side. The shooting had begun again. Situated where he was, John could observe goings on both to the west and the south of their building. When white invaders exposed themselves, John would cut loose with his rifle, firing through the window screens. He told his son that he was "defending Greenwood."

John kept this up for a couple of hours. Before daylight, the whites generally stayed out of Greenwood, but after dawn, their numbers and their determination to enter the black community increased. Hidden as he was, it was some time before the whites found out where John's rifle fire was coming from, but once they did, they started to riddle the building with gunfire. An airplane flew overhead and, probably anxiously, John fired at it. Finally, he told the family that it was time to leave their home. Too many whites were coming.

The family went downstairs and ran north up Greenwood to an undertaker's parlor located about eight buildings away. About ten men were already inside, most of them unarmed. John Williams ran across Greenwood Avenue to Hardy's Pool Hall, where he could get a "right-hand shot" at any whites who were rounding the corner at Greenwood and Archer, or were breaking into his family's home. In the undertaker's parlor, Bill went to the back of the building, which bordered the M.K.T. railroad tracks, to see how close the whites were who were coming from the west. The back of the building, which was quite long, had been rented out for "bawdyhouses and that sort of thing," and behind a partition, he saw a number of people who were intoxicated on opium. Peering out a window, Bill could see whites peeking out from behind railroad cars.

When he got back to the front of the parlor, he found out that his mother had left for her mother's house on Detroit Avenue. His father then called to him from across the street, "We can't get Mama now. They probably won't shoot her. But you come on." Running low, Bill and Hosea crossed Greenwood. Bill could hear bullets singing down the avenue. A man from the undertaker's parlor followed, and they went up to the second floor of the pool hall where John positioned himself and his rifle at its front windows. Whites had already begun breaking in and burning on Archer.

The man from the funeral parlor, unknown to Bill, was without a gun and so decided to make the run back to retrieve the shotgun that John had left at the parlor. Dodging bullets, he made it across the street twice again. Although, like John Williams, the man was a good marksman, he could not load the gun properly, so Bill had to show him. The two men held the pool hall position for about an hour before, once again, it was time to go. Whites had broken into buildings on the west side of Greenwood Avenue, directly across from them.

Bill and his father went down the back stairs of the building which housed the pool hall. Bill hesitated, however, because he did not know where Hosea was. His father said, "We'll split up here, and I'll meet you down on Pine Street." His father started walking north along the Midland Valley railroad tracks. A little while later, Bill started walking north, toward Pine, using the alley between Greenwood and Hartford avenues. He had a couple of shotgun shells in his pocket which he threw away. He had gone about two blocks when he was met by three armed whites. One of them said, "Hold up your hands, nigger."

One day later, after having spent the night at the home of a white projectionist who worked at the Dreamland and who secured his release from Convention Hall, Bill Williams was reunited with his mother and father. Together, they went back to Greenwood.

### III

They found the business district to be a burned-out shell. Their home—the building at Greenwood and Archer which also housed their confectionary—had been looted and burned. Their theater, too, was but bricks and ashes.[2]

What had happened? Overnight, over one thousand homes occupied by blacks had been destroyed in Tulsa. The Greenwood business district had been put to the torch. The city had been placed under martial law. Many, both black and white, had died or were wounded.

IV

The history of the Tulsa race riot is but one chapter in the troubled history of racial violence in America. In terms of density of destruction and ratio of casualties to population, it has probably not been equaled by any riot in the United States in this century. Nevertheless, the Tulsa race riot is not a lone aberration rudely jutting out of a saner, calmer past. Events similar to the one described here are part of the histories of Boston, Providence, New York, Philadelphia, Washington, Atlanta, New Orleans, Detroit, Chicago, Duluth, Omaha, Los Angeles, and scores of other cities and towns in every part of the nation. They were a part of the American scene in the 1830s as well as in one city in the late spring of 1921.[3] The story of Tulsa is very much a story of America.

"What the future holds regarding race relations in America nobody knows," wrote historian William Tuttle in 1970, "but one thing is evident. The optimist cannot take solace in the past."[4] The concerned can, however, learn from it. But to do so, it is necessary to lift the Tulsa race riot from its distorting setting as a singular, "dramatic event," and view it within the context of the various forces which shaped both Tulsa and America in 1921, and which, indeed, shape them both today.

Chapter 1
# Boom
# Cities

I

Tulsa was a boom city in a boom state. Between 1890 and 1920, the population of the land which became the state of Oklahoma increased seven and one-half times; the total population in 1920 was over two million. Thirteen other states and territories, primarily in the West, more than doubled their populations during this period, but Oklahoma's rate of increase was by far the largest. And of these states, only Texas, with its much larger land area, surpassed Oklahoma in the number of people added to her population during these decades. By far, the greater part of Oklahoma's population boom was due to immigration. But unlike the forced immigration of Native Americans which began in the 1830s, the new immigrants' move was a matter of choice. Most of them came between 1890 and 1910, an era marked by land runs and statehood (1907).[1] They came for a variety of reasons and from a variety of places, but for many Oklahoma was a place to start life anew.

Tulsa's growth during the first years of the twentieth century was even more dramatic. Located along a bend in the Arkansas River in a verdant area where the oak-laden foothills of the Ozarks slowly melt westward into the treeless Great Plains, it had been a Creek settlement known as "Tulsey Town" during the latter part of the nineteenth century. The first permanent white settlers did not arrive until the early 1880s; Tulsa's population in 1900 was estimated at

1,390. During the next two decades, the city's population skyrocketed. In 1910, the Census Bureau listed Tulsa's population at 18,182; in 1920 at 72,075. In that latter census, Tulsa ranked as the ninety-seventh largest city in the United States, comparable in size to such cities as San Diego; Wichita; Wilkes-Barre, Pennsylvania; and Troy, New York. City directory estimates, it should be added, were higher than those of the federal government, and the 1921 directory recorded Tulsa's population as 98,874.[2]

The primary reason for Tulsa's rapid growth was oil, and as one writer in the 1920s remarked, "the story of Tulsa is the story of oil." Petroleum had been discovered in 1897 near Bartlesville, Indian Territory, some fifty miles north of Tulsa, and in 1901 the Southwest oil boom seriously got under way with two noted petroleum discoveries: the Spindletop strike near Beaumont, Texas; and the strike at Red Fork, Indian Territory.[3]

The hamlet of Red Fork was located directly across the Arkansas River from Tulsa, and its strike was an important early contributor to the city's growth. Tulsa had been incorporated only three years prior to the Red Fork gusher, and had but few characteristics to distinguish it from other towns in the northeastern part of the territory. It had, however, a hotel of some form as early as 1882, and a local Commercial Club, established in 1902, raised enough money to convince officials of the Missouri, Kansas and Texas Railroad that their line should pass through Tulsa in 1903. A year later, three entrepreneurs opened a toll bridge which they had constructed across the Arkansas River, thus making the Red Fork field more accessible to the business and laboring communities in Tulsa.[4]

Tulsa was growing, but the event which ushered in the city's most spectacular growth did not come until 1905. In the fall of that year, the Ida Glenn No. 1 oil well gushed some fourteen miles from Tulsa. The area near Sapulpa where the strike was made became known as the Glenn Pool, considered to be "the richest small oil field in the world."[5] A veritable forest of derricks was constructed in the area during the next two years, and from some of Glenn Pool's five hundred producing wells flowed more than two thousand barrels of oil per day. Other big oil discoveries followed that of Glenn Pool, and by 1907, the year of statehood, Oklahoma led the nation in oil production. Six years later, Oklahoma was producing one-quarter of all the oil produced in the nation, and by 1915, the young state was producing up to 300,000 barrels of oil per day.

Oklahoma rode on top of its oil boom, and Tulsa more and more became *the city* associated with the boom, the oil industry, and the vast Mid-Continent oil field. After Glenn Pool, the face of Tulsa changed rapidly. A five-story brick hotel with over five hundred rooms was completed one year after the celebrated oil strike of 1905, and civic leaders promoted a "special train called the 'Coal Oil Johnny' which pulled about fifteen coaches, leaving Tulsa in the morning, letting the workers off at the various oil fields in the area, and picking them up in the evening for the return trip to Tulsa."[6]

First Street, Tulsa, Indian Territory; probably just after the turn of the century.
Courtesy of McFarlin Library, University of Tulsa

A scene in the Glenn Pool, south of the city.
Courtesy of McFarlin Library, University of Tulsa

Homes were built to accommodate the city's booming population, and a respectable business district was established downtown. The 1909 Tulsa city directory listed no fewer than 126 oil companies with offices in Tulsa. Two years earlier, the city's first oil refinery had been built.[7] Not only was Tulsa a city where the financial and exploratory ends of a booming oil industry were directed, but it soon became a production and oil well supply center as well. The city also became an important commercial center tied to the state's agricultural industry, which claimed in 1920 about one-half of Oklahoma's work force.[8] "Tulsey Town" had grown into one of the Southwest's largest cities in practically no time at all. Local boosters called it the "Magic City."[9]

The "Magic City." Fourth and Main, looking north, 1918.
Courtesy of McFarlin Library, University of Tulsa

II

Native Americans were the first settlers of the area which was to become Tulsa. The next racial group to be among the area's inhabitants
were not whites, but blacks. Afro-Americans were present in the
Tulsa area probably throughout most of the nineteenth century, as
the Cherokees and the Creeks—who were moved onto what had
been Osage lands beginning in the 1830s—had black slaves. After
the Civil War and the coming of emancipation, black freedmen remained in the area and were not without a voice in the local government. Freedmen in the Coweta District of the Creek Nation, in
which Tulsa was later located, were sometimes chosen for district
public offices. Blacks were also involved in the Green Peach War, a
"serious political disturbance" which broke out among the Creeks
in 1883.[10]

As the nineteenth century waned, and Tulsa grew, the city's
black community became larger and more established. Two black
churches, the Vernon African Methodist Episcopal Church and the
Macedonia Baptist Church, had their foundings in 1895 and 1897, respectively.[11] Immigration no doubt also affected the social life of
black Tulsa, as blacks born in other states became the majority
within the black community. In 1900—when blacks comprised
about 5 percent of the total population of the city—more black
Tulsans had been born in Missouri than in Indian Territory, with

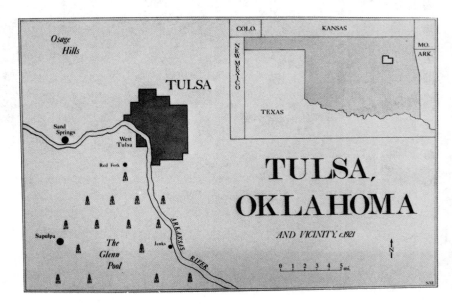

Mississippians and Georgians ranking third and fourth. Most of the adults at that time worked as day laborers, servants, or housewives, but there also was a black lawyer, blacksmith, stonemason, and a full-time preacher. A fair number of the domestic workers "lived-in"

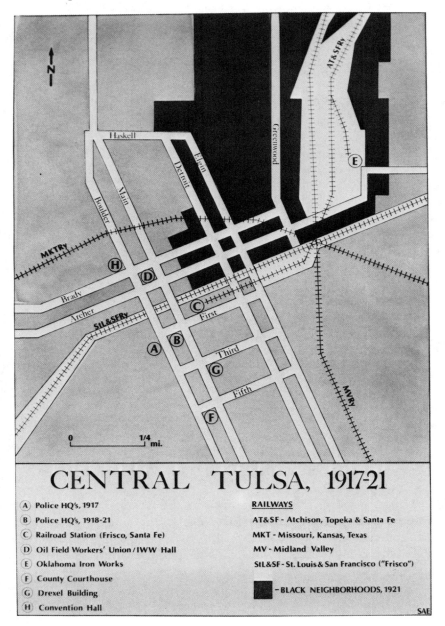

# CENTRAL TULSA, 1917-21

(A) Police HQ's, 1917

(B) Police HQ's, 1918-21

(C) Railroad Station (Frisco, Santa Fe)

(D) Oil Field Workers' Union / IWW Hall

(E) Oklahoma Iron Works

(F) County Courthouse

(G) Drexel Building

(H) Convention Hall

**RAILWAYS**

AT&SF - Atchison, Topeka & Santa Fe

MKT - Missouri, Kansas, Texas

MV - Midland Valley

StL&SF - St. Louis & San Francisco ("Frisco")

■ - BLACK NEIGHBORHOODS, 1921

SAE

with their white employers.[12] As for the others, apparently it was not until 1905 that black Tulsans began to live along Greenwood Avenue in the northeast section of the city, when a strip of land in that area was sold to a group of blacks. One year later—one year before statehood—Tulsa boasted a black newspaper, the Tulsa *Guide*, edited by G. W. Hutchins. And when statehood came, black Tulsa had two doctors, one barber, and three grocers among its business people.[13]

By 1910 the black population had grown to 10 percent of the total population of the city, and there was then at least one black trade union, the Hod Carriers Local No. 199. One year later, Barney Cleaver became Tulsa's first black police officer, and a few years after that the Dreamland Theatre and other black businesses graced Greenwood Avenue. The second lowest black illiteracy rate of any county in Oklahoma testified to the presence of a black school, and over three-fourths of black Tulsa's school-age children were attending school. A new black newspaper, the Tulsa *Weekly Planet*, edited by Professor J. H. Hill, was then in existence.[14]

While black Tulsans were "welcomed" to work at common labor, domestic, and service jobs in any part of the city, they were "not welcome" to patronize white businesses south of the tracks and in other sections of the city. This was a major reason, according to local historian Henry Whitlow, for the growth of Tulsa's black business community, located primarily along Greenwood Avenue.[15] Thus, in the early years of the twentieth century, Tulsa became not one city, but two. Confined by law and by white racism, black Tulsa was a separate city, serving the needs of the black community. And as Tulsa boomed, black Tulsa did too.

By the year of the riot, 1921, the black population had grown to almost 11,000 and the community counted two black schools, Dunbar and Booker T. Washington, one black hospital, and two black newspapers, the Tulsa *Star* and the Oklahoma *Sun*. Black Tulsa at this time had some thirteen churches and three fraternal lodges—Masonic, Knights of Pythias, and I.O.O.F.—plus two black theaters and a black public library.[16]

A focal point of the community was the intersection of Greenwood and Archer. This geographical location—a single corner—has had something of a symbolic life of its own in Tulsa for most of the twentieth century, as it has been a key spot of delineation between the city's black and white worlds. The corner has even been men-

tioned in song. Beginning about 1941, Bob Wills and his Texas Play-
boys, a white "western swing" group which drew their music heavily from black sources, sang:

Would I like to go to Tulsa?
You bet your boots I would,
Let me off at Archer,
I'll walk down to Greenwood

Take me back to Tulsa . . .[17]

And in the 1970s, a nationally known black musical group from
Tulsa, the Gap Band, drew its name from Greenwood, Archer, and
Pine streets.

The first two blocks of Greenwood Avenue north of Archer were
known as "Deep Greenwood." It comprised the heart of Tulsa's
black business community, and was known by some before the riot
as the "Negro's Wall Street," while an organizer for the National
Negro Business League visiting black Tulsa in 1913 called it "a regu-
lar Monte Carlo." Two- and three-story brick buildings lined the avenue, housing a variety of commercial establishments, including a
dry goods store, two theaters, groceries, confectionaries, restaurants,
and billiard halls. A number of black Tulsa's eleven rooming houses

Greenwood Avenue looking north from Archer, *ca.* 1918.
Courtesy of W. D. Williams

and four hotels were located here. "Deep Greenwood" was also a favorite place for the offices of Tulsa's unusually large number of black lawyers, doctors, and other professionals. The district would especially come alive on Thursday nights and Sunday afternoons and evenings—the traditional "days off" for black domestic workers living in white neighborhoods.[18]

On some of the side streets adjacent to the famed avenue was the world of poverty that some black Tulsans shared with their racial brethren throughout America. In addition to the shanties and houses made from the wood of packing crates, one would also find black Tulsa's share of prostitution houses, speakeasies, and "choc" joints. "Choc" is short for Choctaw beer, a thick, milky-colored intoxicant made from Choctaw root, or Indian hemp—unrelated to marijuana—which was quite popular with more than a few black, red, and white Tulsans at the time, as well as in later years.[19]

Along Detroit Avenue and certain other streets were the neat, sturdy homes of some of those black Tulsans who owned businesses lining Greenwood Avenue, augmented by the houses of the city's black professional class. Within this elite group, some were rumored to have assets in excess of $100,000.[20] Not all black Tulsans lived in the Greenwood district, however. Many lived in "white" neighborhoods where they worked as servants and housekeepers for well-to-do white families. They usually resided in "quarters" located on their employers' lots, generally above or next to garages, and their visits to Greenwood would primarily be to shop or attend church or school.[21]

While "Deep Greenwood" was assuredly one of the finest black commercial districts in the entire Southwest, it was scarcely free from white influence and control. Whites owned a large portion of the land in the district. Furthermore, black Tulsa's service-oriented businesses were geared toward catering a wage-earning population. Few of them employed more than a handful of people. Economically, black Tulsa was dependent upon the wages paid to black workers by white employers. Despite its visible solidity of brick, Greenwood rested upon an uncertain economic foundation reflecting ominous social and racial realities.[22]

Chapter 2
# Race Relations and
# Local Violence

I

Whereas Tulsa's growth in the early twentieth century was virtually unmatched by any other American city, Tulsa's race riot was far from being the only event of its kind in the nation. Indeed, the happenings in Tulsa in the spring of 1921 are incomprehensible without some familiarity with the currents in American race relations and racial ideologies of that time. Not only must the riot be viewed within that context, but also within that of three crucial events of violence and threatened violence—racial and nonracial—which occurred in Tulsa during the four preceding years.

Beginning in 1917, a series of race riots broke out across America which culminated in the summer of 1919, ushering in what Tulsa-bred historian John Hope Franklin has described as "the greatest period of inter-racial strife the nation ever witnessed." These riots took place in Minnesota, Nebraska, Illinois, and Pennsylvania, as well as in the South. Perhaps their clearest common denominator was the invasion of black neighborhoods by whites. The race riot in Tulsa was the last one in this "series": it has not until the Harlem riot of 1935 and the Detroit incident of 1943 that racial violence on the scale of the 1919-era riots was repeated.[1]

We can get some idea of the racial climate from the fact that in the year of the Tulsa riot fifty-nine blacks were lynched in southern or "border" states. The alleged causes for these lynchings ranged from murder to making "improper remarks to [a] white woman," to being *a relative* of someone who was lynched. Although the number of lynchings per year in the United States during the first decades of the twentieth century decreased from those reached in the 1890s, the degree of barbarity in these lynchings had generally increased. The burning of live victims was not uncommon in twentieth-century southern "lynchings," a fact which made the United States one of the few nations in the world at that time where human beings were burned at the stake.[2] During the very weeks that saw black Tulsa torn apart, a lynching in Moultrie, Georgia, was described in vivid detail by a correspondent of the Washington *Eagle*:

> Immediately a cracker by the name of Ken Murphy gave the Confederate yell: 'Whoo-whoo—let's get the nigger.' Simultaneously five hundred poor pecks rushed on the armed sheriffs, who made no resistance whatever. They tore the Negro's clothing off before he was placed in a waiting automobile. This was done in broad daylight. The Negro was unsexed and made to eat a portion of his anatomy which had been cut away. Another portion was sent by parcel post to Governor Dorsey, whom the people of this section hate bitterly.
>
> The Negro was taken to a grove, where each one of more than five hundred people, in Ku Klux ceremonial, had placed a pine nut around a stump, making a pyramid to the height of ten feet. The Negro was chained to a stump and asked if he had anything to say. Castrated and in indescribable torture, the Negro asked for a cigarette, lit it and blew the smoke in the face of his tormentors.
>
> The pyre was lit and a hundred men and women, old and young, grandmothers among them, joined hands and danced while the Negro burned. A big dance was held in a barn nearby that evening in celebration of the burning, many people coming by automobile from nearby cities to the gala event.[3]

Black Americans were losing ground during this era in other ways, too. Many black postal employees lost their jobs during Woodrow Wilson's administration, and the number of black police declined. In the organized labor movement, once in 1917 and twice in 1921, resolutions to denounce racial discrimination in union locals were defeated in conventions of the American Federation of Labor. And hotels and restaurants in northern cities like Boston and Chicago which had previously served blacks had begun to bar them.[4]

These national trends were mirrored by similar developments in Oklahoma, but their effects in the young state were even more disastrous because of the unique history of race relations in the territory. The character of Native American slavery had been debated back and forth, and although even the mildest form of slavery is a far cry from freedom, one "Creek Negro" is recorded as stating: "I was eating out of the same pot with the Indians . . . while they were still licking the master's boots in Texas." Beginning in the 1880s, there had been an attempt to make Oklahoma into an all-black state—a dream of Edwin P. McCabe, former state auditor of Kansas, and by those southern blacks who formed "Oklahoma Clubs" during the land rush era—and in 1890, a black had been elected to the territorial legislature.[5] During the next three decades, a virtual war was waged as to whether Oklahoma would conform to the national pattern of race relations, and most of the results of this conflict proved to be particularly catastrophic to black Oklahomans—to those for whom Oklahoma was their native land, as well as to those who had risked so much to come and try to make it into a Canaan for themselves and their children.[6]

Beginning in the 1890s, the territorial government passed its first Jim Crow laws. Although certain similar measures were defeated in the twentieth century, others were added, and Oklahoma was later to have the distinction of being the first state to segregate its telephone booths. Oklahoma's greatest racist distinction in Jim Crow legislation, however, concerned the franchise. Up until 1910, black Oklahomans legally had the right to vote, and it appears that many of them exercised that right. But that year—which also saw the last black to sit in the Oklahoma State Legislature until 1964—the infamous "Grandfather Clause" was adopted by the legislature, and it effectively disfranchised the state's black population. Although it was ruled unconstitutional by the Supreme Court in 1915, a new method, that of setting "an extremely brief registration period for voters not already eligible," was adopted to check black suffrage. In Tulsa, and other places, blacks did however continue to vote.[7]

The first two decades of the twentieth century brought an increase in racial violence to Oklahoma and by 1911 the nature of lynchings in the state began to change: thereafter, more blacks were lynched per year than whites. And although fewer blacks were lynched in the state from 1917 to 1919 than in the preceding three years, the war was by no means a definite improver of the status of blacks in the state. For one thing, the death blow which the war years dealt to the Oklahoma Socialist party, the Industrial Workers of the World (IWW), and other radical groups in the state was not without significance to black Oklahomans as a group. The IWW had been founded as an interracial body, and its national office rhetorically supported black rights. The Oklahoma Socialist party "fought consistently for full enfranchisement of Negroes," it has been claimed, and there were black party members. The Socialist party in Tulsa had never been as strong as it was elsewhere in the state, and after 1918, Socialist slates of candidates for city offices were no longer being fielded by the party local.[8]

Nationwide, the resurgence of aggressive white supremacy was accompanied by a racist literature so ubiquitous that one historian concluded that the "chief difficulty in studying racist attitudes towards Negroes during the early twentieth century is the existence of mountains of readily available materials." One such book was Madison Grant's *The Passing of the Great Race*, which another historian has called the central intellectual inspiration of the white racism of the 1920s. Totally ignorant of black history, Grant stated that "negroes have demonstrated throughout recorded time that they do not possess the potentiality of progress or initiative from within." A similar work referred to black Americans as "ten million malignant cancers [which] gnaw the vitals of our body politic."[9]

The most widespread organizational means for the expression of white racist and nativist thought was the so-called "second" or "revived" Ku Klux Klan. Organized in 1915, it was particularly active in the 1920s. Klansmen were found throughout the nation, from Maine to Oregon and from Florida to California. Blacks, however, were not the only victims of Klan terrorism and intimidation; Jews, Catholics, immigrants, and those whom the hooded order felt to be guilty of moral turpitude (for alleged "crimes" such as adultery or bootlegging) were also victimized. The Klan was very strong in the Southwest, and particularly in Tulsa, which boasted by the time of the riot a "thriving chapter." Late in 1921, the Tulsa "Klan No. 2" claimed a

# Americans Gather Under The Fiery Cross on The Rolling Prairies of Oklahoma

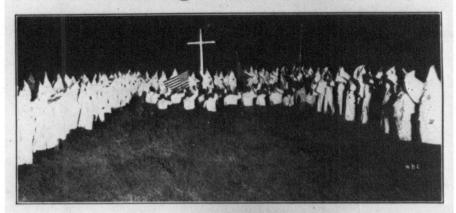

OUT ON the rolling Oklahoma prairie the Fiery Cross, symbol of the Klan, testifies to the alien world that Americans are on guard and alert to safeguard this country's sacred heritage.

The photograph is of a ceremonial and naturalization conducted by Twin Elk Klan Number 146, Realm of Oklahoma, a few nights ago. Twin Elk Klan is at Hobart, Oklahoma, and is one of the live wire organizations in that section of the realm.

A score of aliens are shown kneeling before the American Flag and the Fiery Cross, taking the sacred oath which makes them citizens of the Invisible Empire. Five thousand curious people witnessed the Klan ceremonies from afar.

Klan ceremony, Hobart, Oklahoma.
Courtesy of the Western History Collections, University of Oklahoma Library

Swearing in new Klansmen in Oklahoma. Tulsa was one of the state's strongest Klan centers.
Courtesy of the Western History Collections, University of Oklahoma Library

membership of 3,200. Moreover, the Women of the Ku Klux Klan were also said to be "thriving" in Tulsa soon after this separate order was founded in June, 1923. Furthermore, Tulsa was to have the distinction of being one of the few places where the "Junior" Ku Klux Klan existed. This order, founded in 1924, was open to white boys from twelve to eighteen years of age.[10]

In the latter months of 1921, "masked bands" whipped at least thirteen persons in Tulsa County. County officials eschewed making inquiries into these beatings on the grounds that the victims "probably got what they deserved and that formal investigations would only bring criticism to the investigators." Such an official stance, of course, amounted to an "open invitation" to the Klan for further extralegal acts of violence. As might be expected in such an environment, the influence of the Klan became notably pronounced. As one authority has written, "In Tulsa County the Klan could not lose." In the November 1922 elections, for example, both the Republican and Democratic candidates for county attorney and sheriff were Klansmen.[11]

Recruiting for World War I, downtown Tulsa.

Courtesy of the Tulsa County Historical Society.

II

How did black Tulsans—and black Americans in general—cope with this increasingly oppressive racial climate? How were they to respond to yet another period of heightened white violence? Many concurred with one black veteran from Chicago who, in describing his postwar outlook, stated: "I ain't looking for trouble, but if it comes my way I ain't dodging."[12]

Participation in the First World War had indeed helped to clarify black thinking on the subject of white militancy. The fact that black soldiers had fought and died in France only added to black America's indignation toward the sharp postwar wave of white violence. During the war, Dr. W. E. B. Du Bois of the National Association for the Advancement of Colored People (NAACP) had urged in *Crisis*: "Let us, while this war lasts, forget our special grievances and close our ranks shoulder to shoulder with our white citizens and the allied nations that are fighting for democracy." A year later, however, in September of 1919, *Crisis* stated: "To-day we raise the terrible weapon of Self-Defense. When the murderer comes, he shall no longer strike us in the back. When the armed lynchers gather, we too must gather armed. When the mob moves, we propose to meet it with bricks and clubs and guns." *Crisis* did, though, advise its readers to "tread here in solemn caution" and not to "seek reform by violence."[13] In a similar vein, Marcus Garvey chaired a convention of the Universal Negro Improvement Association which resolved in 1920 that "the Negro should adopt every means to protect himself against barbarous practices inflicted upon him because of his color."[14]

This concept of self-defense was voiced in a number of other black periodicals and by numerous other black leaders. Some were quite militant. The *Wisconsin Weekly Blade* stated that one "cannot be too radical in a righteous cause." Black socialist leader A. Philip Randolph, noting that Anglo-Saxon jurisprudence recognized the law of self-defense, concluded that blacks should employ armed force against white assailants, and black journalist John Edward Bruce resolved that "equality is not obtained by gift but by struggle."[15]

At times, black spokesmen combined religious references with desperate visions of apocalypse. In October, 1919, *Challenge Magazine* of New York editorialized:

> America hates, lynches, enslaves us not because we are black, but because we are weak. A strong, united Negro race will not be mistreated any more than a strong united Japanese race. It is always strength over weakness, might over right.
> But with education comes thought, with thought comes action; with action comes freedom.
> Read! Read! Read! Then when the mob comes, whether with torch or with gun, let us stand at Armageddon and battle for the Lord.[16]

Black religious leaders, it should be added, were far from quiescent on these issues. For example, when a number of black Methodist bishops were asked to condemn the use of violence in 1919, many of them "answered that self-restraint and patience should be practised, but that if white assailants would not desist, Negroes should use arms if necessary to protect themselves and their homes."[17]

Black Tulsans were not unaffected by these intellectual currents which swept across black America during this period. Both W. E. B Du Bois and Chief Alfred Sam—a black leader who advocated a return of American blacks to Africa—spoke in Tulsa before the race riot. There had been interest in forming an NAACP chapter in Tulsa at least as early as 1917, and black organizations in the city prior to the riot included a local chapter of the militant African Blood Brotherhood (ABB). With branches scattered throughout the United States and the Caribbean, the ABB proposed that "Blacks organize into trade unions, build cooperatively owned businesses, and create paramilitary units to safeguard the community." And black Tulsa, it should be added, had its share of World War I veterans, some of whom had fought in France.[18]

Similarly, extant issues of Tulsa's black press reveal a concern with the problems confronting black Americans nationwide—including that of black responses to white violence. Although differences of opinion existed, one editorial in the Tulsa *Star* in 1920 spoke for a large segment of the city's black community on that problem. In the editorial, entitled "Misguided Oklahoma Patriots," the newspaper was critical of an armed group of Oklahoma City blacks who had gathered after a black had been lynched by whites.

Although the *Star* stated that it was the paper's aim "to seek honorable and peaceful ways of settling the differences which unavoidably now and then crop up between the races," the newspaper added that "it is quite evident that the proper time to afford protection to any prisoner is BEFORE and during the time he is being lynched."[19] Thus, clearly, there were black Tulsans who were not "looking for trouble," but were not about to "dodge" should it come their way.

### III

And there was no dearth of "trouble" in Tulsa during the years immediately preceding the race riot. In particular, three incidents warrant our attention, for each of them previewed elements which were to be at work in the spring of 1921. They occurred in 1917, 1919, and 1920, and although only one of them involved racial violence *per se*, collectively they form a vital section of the necessary backdrop against which the events of the riot must be seen.

The first episode began at about four o'clock in the morning on October 29, 1917, when the home of J. Edgar Pew, a wealthy oil man, was bombed in Tulsa. Although Pew, his wife, and son escaped unharmed, the blast did considerable damage to the house, demolishing the front porch and blowing the front wall of the house inward. Pew was vice-president of the Carter Oil Company, a major subsidiary of Standard Oil.[20] Four hours later, an oil worker named W. J. Powers was arrested at the Frisco train station, but was not charged with the bombing, pending an investigation. Later that day, the chief of police, E. L. Lucas, offered the opinion that the attack on the Pew home "is the first in a series of depredidations [*sic*] in a gigantic plot to destroy the property of the oil companies and the residences of the leaders in the oil business in the Mid Continent field."[21]

In the same spirit, the Tulsa *World*—one of the city's three major white newspapers at the time—claimed to have evidence from "unimpeachable sources" to implicate the Industrial Workers of the World (IWW), in a story which carried the headline, "I.W.W. PLOT BREAKS PREMATURELY IN BLOWING UP OF PEW RESIDENCE." The newspaper claimed that members of the IWW had been sent to Tulsa from all over the country, and that the "danger cannot be exaggerated." As for Powers, the *World* reported that he was "caught trying to leave town," and that his "excited haste" in denying IWW membership "confirmed the belief of the detectives that he is a member." Furthermore, the newspaper claimed: "The *World* is one of the institutions marked for destruction. Four letters have been received in the past four weeks from I.W.W.'s and in each one reference is made to the 'certain downfall of capitalist newspapers.' The *World* is ready for them."[22]

The authorities investigating the case claimed to have but few clues, and felt that the bomb plot may have originated in Muskogee.[23] While the story briefly died in the city's other newspapers, the *World* continued its attack on the IWW. In an October 31 editorial entitled "Patience Has an End," the newspaper endorsed vigilante solutions, likening political radicals to horse thieves and recommending similar treatment: "Why should any discrimination be made between a horse thief and one of these cowardly vandals." Elsewhere in the same issue, the *World*—no longer claiming to have any evidence linking the IWW to the Pew bombing—was even more explicit in its final solution to the IWW.

> Right here is a good place to disagree with the statement, frequently expressed by Oklahoma editors, that the I.W.W.'s and other pro-Hun individuals should "leave the country." As a matter of fact, there is no place for them to go. The only relief is a wholesale application of concentration camps. Or, what is hemp worth now, the long foot?[24]

Such extravagant anxiety on the part of the *World* was traceable, in part, to the continuing presence of political radicalism in Oklahoma, a phenomenon evident in the Populist uprising in the 1890s and superseded by a strong socialist presence in the state in the first decades of the twentieth century, of which the Industrial Workers of the World was a part. That the IWW was not pro-German, but was rather against the war, did not seem to concern the *World* in its journalistic campaign against them.[25] Yet, there was an even more important reason for the newspaper's vehemence against the organization. It had to do with the fact that the Tulsa IWW office, which had been set up at the New Fox Building on Brady Street in January, 1917, was a local of the IWW-affiliated Oil Field Workers' Union (OFWU), and the union had reportedly organized some three hundred oil workers in the Tulsa area under the IWW banner. The prospect of the Mid-Continent oil field's being completely organized by the OFWU was more than a prowar, pro-oil-company newspaper such as the *World* was willing to tolerate.[26]

A week after the Pew bombing, the Tulsa police raided the IWW hall on Brady Street, finding the men inside "seated about the place, playing cards and reading." The local secretary was receiving dues from some members "and placing stamps in their membership books." When the secretary informed the police—who had immediately begun to search the hall—that the men were paying rent for the hall and asked to see a search warrant, the head of the police raiding party "replied he did not give a damn if we were paying rent for four places [as] they would search them whenever they felt like it." The men inside offered no resistance and, though no incriminating evidence was found, the eleven men present were arrested and placed under the highest bond Oklahoma law permitted. One prisoner was a local printer and another worked as a plumber for the Monarch Plumbing Company. Neither of these two men could possibly have been guilty of vagrancy, which was the charge lodged.[27]

The *World* declared that with the raid, "War on the I.W.W. was de-

A scene in the Mid-Continent field, south of the city. Tulsa's IWW chapter sought to organize the region's oil workers into the Oil Field Workers Union.

clared by the city of Tulsa last night." This was indeed the case, if the newspaper was referring to Tulsa's municipal government. The union men were political prisoners in a city where many looked with disdain at the current oil workers' strike in Texas and Louisiana, a strike which some alleged to have been influenced by the IWW.[28] Police Captain Wilkerson, who led the raid, stated: "Regardless of the outcome of the cases, we are going to arrest every man who is found loitering about the I.W.W. headquarters. If they get out of jail and go back there we will arrest them again, and again and again. Tulsa is not big enough to hold any traitors during our government's crisis, and the sooner these fellows get out of town the better for them."[29] Wilkerson's words proved to be true. The next evening, police detectives raided the IWW hall once again, and arrested the one man who was there, who soon joined the other eleven in the city jail. (One of the twelve had provided for bail, but his bondsman backed out, leaving him incarcerated.)[30]

Commenting on the upcoming case, the *World* stated: "There is much speculation today whether any attorney in Tulsa would risk attracting the contempt of loyal citizens by appearing in court today to represent the defendants." Tulsa attorney Charles Richardson apparently decided to risk that contempt. Prior to the trial, Richardson stated that certain acts of misconduct needed to have occurred for a vagrancy charge, and as these had not happened, the men should be freed. "What we are going to prove," he said, "is that this I.W.W. is the only fraternal society in the country which requires that every man, before being accepted, shall establish the fact that he is a bonafide worker and wage earner."[31]

During the first day of the trial, attorneys for the prosecution sought to learn the attitude of the defendants and witnesses about the government. When asked his opinion on this subject, E. M. Boyd, secretary of the local IWW chapter, replied, "We are not interested in that, we are interested in raising wages." A pipeline worker, Boyd stated that eighteen years ago he earned three dollars a day for his work, and that today, he made the same amount. After five hours, Judge T. D. Evans adjourned the court until the next afternoon.[32] (Evans later became the mayor of Tulsa, and held that office during the race riot.)

T. D. Evans, judge at the 1917
IWW trial, and mayor of Tulsa
during the race riot.
Courtesy of the Office of the Mayor, City of Tulsa

The *World*, disappointed that "nothing sensational had happened"
thus far at the trial, could not conceal its impatience. In an editorial
entitled "Get Out the Hemp" which appeared the next morning, the
newspaper—which was then edited by Eugene Lorton—advised:

> If the I.W.W. or its twin brother, the Oil Workers Union, gets busy in your
> neighborhood, kindly take occasion to decrease the supply of hemp. A
> knowledge of how to tie a knot that will stick might come handy in a few
> days. It is no time to dally with the enemies of the country. The unre-
> stricted production of petroleum is as necessary to the winning of the war
> as the unrestricted production of gunpowder. We are either going to whip
> Germany or Germany is going to whip us. The first step in the whipping
> of Germany is to strangle the I.W.W.'s. Kill 'em just as you would kill any
> other kind of snake. Don't scotch 'em; kill 'em. And kill 'em dead. It is no
> time to waste money on trials and continuances like that. All is neces-
> sary is the evidence and a firing squad. Probably the carpenters union will
> contribute the timber for the coffins.[33]

The IWW was not without supporters, however, as was revealed in
the continuation of the trial that evening. F. J. Ryan, a former IWW
local secretary who had also been involved in the Free Speech fight
led by the Socialist party of Tulsa in 1914, was applauded by court-

room spectators for his statements on decreasing wages and soaring prices. He added his opinion that the case was fixed and that he knew for a fact that posters were at that moment being printed ordering the IWW to leave town. Judge Evans found it necessary to instruct police detectives in the courtroom to arrest anyone who applauded further.[34]

The trial was brought to a speedy conclusion. Not only did Judge Evans find the twelve guilty, fine them $100 each, and commit them to jail, but he had five people in the courtroom who had served as witnesses for the defense (including Ryan) arrested, tried on the spot, and also declared guilty. The police were then instructed to transfer the seventeen prisoners that night to the county jail, located in the county courthouse.[35]

One half hour later, between eleven and midnight, nine police officers began to escort the seventeen prisoners to the county jail. But en route, at the intersection of First Street and Boulder Avenue, the caravan was halted by a group of forty or fifty armed men garbed in "long black robes and black masks," who called themselves the "Knights of Liberty." These men bound the hands and feet of the seventeen prisoners, and had the police drive them to a secluded ravine west of the city near Irving Place.[36]

The ravine was lit by a fire and by the headlights of automobiles drawn in a circle. The seventeen union men were then stripped to the waist, tied to a tree, and whipped. With each stroke of the whip—which, according to one of the union men was "a double piece of new rope, five-eighths or three-quarters hemp"—the black-robed leader of the "Knights of Liberty" was to have said, "In the name of the outraged women and children of Belgium." Hot tar and feathers were then applied to the bloodied backs of the seventeen men. One prisoner, an older man, pleaded with the "Knights": "I have lived here for eighteen years, and have raised a large family. I am not an I.W.W. I am as patriotic as any man here." But he too was whipped. Several of the prisoners, however, defiantly proclaimed their allegiance to the IWW. F. J. Ryan, the former local secretary, was whipped twice, the second time leaving the hot tar imbedded in his back.[37]

After their torture, the seventeen prisoners were directed toward

## Capital and Labor Are Partners—Not Enemies

*John D. Rockefeller, Jr.*

IWW periodicals were quick to point out to their readers that the real cause of the violence against their members—by conservative vigilantes during the war under the guise of patriotism—was economic. This cartoon appeared in *One Big Union Monthly*, March 1, 1919. Note the "Tulsa" skull at right.

the Osage Hills and told to leave. Rifle and pistol volleys, shot into the air, sped their flight. Three hours later, the seventeen union men found refuge at the cabin of "an I.W.W. friend" and cleansed their wounds of the tar and feathers. Meanwhile, the police were "taken" back to town from the ravine. That same evening, printed signs appeared at various points around the city of Tulsa, including the train station, on telephone poles, at the IWW hall, and on the door to the law office of Charles Richardson, who had defended the accused men. The signs read:

> NOTICE TO I.W.W.'S. DON'T LET THE SUN SET ON YOU IN TULSA.
> —Vigilance Committee[38]

The tangible evidence is conclusive that the Tulsa police worked in close concert with the "Knights of Liberty." Though Chief of Police Lucas stated later that his men were "powerless" against the masked men, and that every precaution had been taken to protect the prisoners, the nine police officers who comprised the escort were surely armed, as even traffic policemen in Tulsa carried guns at the time. Indeed, had they not been armed, given the circumstances, that in itself would constitute prima facie evidence of police collusion. That the police and the "Knights" worked together is further born out by a statement made later by one of the whipped men:

> It was very evident that the police force knew what was going to happen when they took us from jail, as there were extra gowns and masks provided *which were put on by the Chief of Police and one detective named——, and the number of blows we received were regulated by the Chief of Police himself who was easily recognizable by six of us at least.* It was all prearranged. The police knew where we were going, or the extra gowns and masks would not have been ready for the Chief and——.[39]

Apparently, the chief of police was not the only well-known individual involved in the affair, for John Moran, deputy U.S. marshal in charge of the Tulsa office, later stated, "You would be surprised at the prominent men in town who were in this mob."[40]

Not surprisingly, the local authorities took no action against the "Knights of Liberty." The county attorney was out of town. The city attorney stated that although he deplored the incident, he was "powerless to proceed in the case, owing to the fact that it was not covered by any city ordinance." The police said that they could not identify any of the "Knights." They had other quarry. According to the *World*, two days after the flogging, the police, said the paper, "are continuing their search for I.W.W.'s and will arrest them as fast as they are discovered." Indeed, when one of the seventeen whipped men reached nearby Sand Springs and was arrested by the chief of police there, authorities in Tulsa told the chief to "turn him loose and tell him to keep going—away from Tulsa." The Tulsa IWW hall on Brady Street was closed down.[41]

In the aftermath of the incident, the *World*—whose editorials had urged a far more serious fate for the union men than that which they received—could barely mask its approval for what had transpired. "As regrettable as the deportation of some very persistent and incorrigible agitators may seem," the newspaper stated, "it may yet prove a deterrent to any ambitious souls anxious to follow their example." The next day, the *World* referred to the "Knights of Liberty" as a "patriotic body," although reminding the reader that some Tulsans were unsure of their methods. Other white newspapers in the city generally concurred with the attitude of the *World*. One paper referred to the event as the "Tulsa Tar Party" and a reporter for the Tulsa *Democrat* also dubbed the tar and feathering "a party, a real American party."[42]

### IV

The 1917 IWW incident revealed how disastrous the consequences could be for a group of Tulsans if the power of an influential newspaper, the city government, and the local courts and police was brought to bear against them. More than that, it revealed how dire the results could be even in such a situation when the defendants were *white* and when the official charge lodged against them was no more serious than vagrancy.[43]

A second incident which contributed to the mob-rule potentialities in Tulsa took place two years later. It had its beginnings at about nine o'clock on the evening of St. Patrick's Day, March 17, 1919, when a white ironworker by the name of O. W. Leonard was accosted by two armed men on the streets of Tulsa. They told him to raise his hands, and when he refused, he was shot in the back. He died twelve hours later in a local hospital. But before he died, Leonard told the authorities that his two assailants were black, and he was able to give the police a very meager description of them.[44]

In its initial coverage of the incident, the *Democrat* stated: "Violence is feared if the guilty pair is taken in charge. Officers are preparing to evade such violence." Yet, although the crime was front-page news, the reporting of the white Tulsa press—the *World*, the *Times*, and the *Democrat*—was mild in comparison to the tone of the IWW coverage two years earlier.[45]

In the days that followed, three black men were arrested in the case and—after employees of the Oklahoma Ironworks had quit work to attend the funeral of their slain co-worker—rumors began to spread in Greenwood that there might be an attempt to lynch the three black defendants. Near midnight on the day after Leonard's funeral, a party of about fifteen armed blacks drove down to the city jail to investigate the situation firsthand. Their leader asked to see if the defendants were safe. "In the meantime," the Tulsa *Times* later reported, "the report of race riot had spread through the streets,"

Tulsa's Black Veterans of World War I. Photograph from the Tulsa *Star*, November 23, 1918.

and, all told, eventually some two hundred black Tulsans had gathered outside of the jail. After temporarily disarming a spokesman for the group, Sergeant Rice of the police department allowed this person to enter the jail and, "see for himself that none of their race had suffered anything, and the men went away, declaring they were satisfied."[46]

The next morning, several blacks went downtown to see if they could get any or all of the prisoners released, but were informed that the sheriff would have formal charges lodged against the prisoners before nightfall. That day the *Democrat* reported that "excitement following the visit of the negro crowd at the police station Thursday night subsided to some extent Friday morning, although much talk of trouble with the colored element was heard."[47]

Actually, the reverse happened—black police officers had trouble with whites. On Saturday night, March 22, a mass meeting was held in Greenwood to discuss ways of suppressing the lawlessness that had been prevalent in the area. On their way from that meeting, shortly before midnight, three black policemen—Barney Cleaver, James Cherry, and Stanley Webb—were held up and fired upon by two white gunmen as they drove past the Oklahoma Ironworks.

The Tulsa police force, *ca.* 1918–1920. Note the two black officers at left.

Aided by two night watchmen at the plant, the three police officers returned the fire, wounding two white men, who were later captured and ultimately accused of being part of a local crime ring.[48] After this week of turmoil, the time of extralegal peril for the three black defendants arrested in connection with the Leonard affair had passed. There was no lynching.

In the aftermath of the incident. Reverend J. H. Abernathy, the black pastor of the First Baptist Church in Greenwood, criticized those black Tulsans who had gone down to the jail on Thursday evening. "I have inquired carefully for the names of the ringleaders from people I know to be reliable," Abernathy stated, "and I have been unable to learn of one of them. The wage earning colored people of Tulsa had little if anything to do with that affair." He described the unknown blacks who visited the jail as "floaters who have drifted in here," and he suggested that "it would be a good thing if we could have a law to compel such people to get out or get to work." Abernathy concluded with this remark: "I don't think that the white citizens of Tulsa would be guilty of the crime this mob was afraid would be committed."[49]

## V

Unlike the IWW prisoners, the three men held in conjunction with the Leonard case were not subjected to the high-pitched abuse of a sensationalistic press nor, to our knowledge, to any extralegal violence. Yet, like the 1917 affair, the events of 1919 revealed much about the nature of law enforcement in Tulsa during the World War I era. Perhaps most importantly, it revealed that there were serious doubts in the black community as to whether the local white law enforcement establishment could be relied upon to protect prisoners, and that there were black Tulsans who were prepared to help protect incarcerated blacks if it was felt that they were in danger of being lynched. The Leonard incident did not, however, close the book on the matter of lynchings and extralegal violence in the "Magic City."

Tulsa police officials variously described the "hi-jacking" and murder of Homer Nida, a twenty-five-year-old white taxi driver, as "the arch murder plot of this city," and "the most cold-blooded act ever committed in the Southwest." At about 9:30 P.M. on Saturday night, August 21, 1920, Nida was employed by two white men and one white woman in front of the Hotel Tulsa to drive them to a dance in Red Fork. En route to the destination, while driving along the Tulsa-Sapulpa highway, Nida became suspicious of his passengers, and he pulled into a gas station where he secreted away some money which he was carrying. Back on the highway, just before they reached Red Fork, Nida was clubbed on the head by one of the men with a revolver.[50] He was then pulled into the back seat of his large Hudson cab, while one of his abductors took the wheel. The party passed through Red Fork, and Nida pleaded for his life, telling the party to take his car and his money, but to spare him. But near the Texas Company's tank farm just outside of Sapulpa, Nida was shot in the stomach and thrown from the car, which sped off down the highway.[51]

A few minutes later, Nida was discovered by a Red Fork garage owner who, with the help of another man, rushed the wounded taxi driver to a Tulsa hospital. While conscious, Nida told the police at the hospital what had happened, and that he could identify the party who had robbed and shot him. He insisted that the woman had no real part in the crime.[52]

The crime and events related to it were made front-page news in the city's two white dailies, the *World* and the *Tribune*. It was also carried by the Tulsa *Star*, which was then the city's black weekly. Other local crimes, including the near fatal stabbing of a truck driver, were relegated to the back pages of the *World* and the *Tribune*, but the papers kept the city posted almost daily on the Nida affair, generally on the front page. The truck driver, one Walter Allen, was stabbed the week before Nida was shot, yet this event received relatively little press play, regardless of the striking parallels that Allen and Nida languished in hospital beds simultaneously and that neither was expected to survive. Indeed, with a wealth of local crimes to choose from, the *World* and the *Tribune* devoted a disproportionate amount of attention to the Nida affair.[53]

On Sunday, the day after Nida was shot, an eighteen-year-old white former telephone company worker named Roy Belton secured a ride from Tulsa to Nowata, a town about fifty miles away. In the car, one of the passengers read aloud the *Tribune's* account of the crime. Belton remarked that he knew who the woman was in Nida's cab, as he had heard her plan the hijacking earlier. The passengers in the car then became suspicious of Belton, and upon reaching Nowata, they informed the local authorities there, who arrested him and had him taken back to Tulsa.[54]

In Tulsa, Belton was taken to Nida's hospital room, where Nida identified Belton as the man who had shot him. Belton, however, denied that he had any knowledge of the crime, and insisted that he had spent Saturday evening with Marie Harmon, a white woman in her twenties. Harmon was arrested by the police, and on Monday she confessed that she had been in Nida's cab with Belton, and a man named George Moore. She claimed that Belton had shot Nida, but that she had known nothing about the plans for the crime.[55]

On Tuesday, Belton confessed. He claimed, however, that the shooting of Nida was unintentional, that the revolver had been damaged when he struck the taxi driver with it, and that it accidentally discharged while he was trying to repair it. Belton, too, stated that Harmon had known nothing about the plans for the crime, but that Raymond Sharp, a seventeen-year-old grocery store employee, did. Sharp was later picked up by the police as an accessory, and he confessed his knowledge of the affair. George Moore, the other man in the cab, was nowhere to be found.[56]

It was reported by the *World* that Belton, "realizing the seriousness of his predicament and bitterly resentful of the manner in which the public had taken the event of Saturday night, asked assurance that violence would not follow his statement." Belton, however, was far from being the only one aware of this possibility. By Thrusday night, August 26, Sheriff Woolley had heard rumors that the courthouse—where Belton, Harmon, and Sharp were interned in the county jail—might be mobbed in the event that Homer Nida died. Consequently, Woolley posted two extra armed guards to protect the three prisoners, who were held on the top floor of the building.[57]

The next day, the *Tribune*, which at that time rather rarely printed

Tulsa courthouse. Most prisoners were held in the jail on its top floor.

front-page photographs, carried one each of Belton and Harmon. The newspaper reported that, in Harmon's case, "the chances are that she will turn state's evidence in the hope that she will escape heavy punishment by so doing." As for Belton, the *Tribune* stated that he planned to "escape on a plea of insanity."[58]

Early on Saturday morning, Homer Nida died. The same day, Roy Belton and Raymond Sharp were arraigned in court, and each pleaded not guilty to the charges. That afternoon's *Tribune* quoted Nida's widow as stating: "I hope that justice will be done for they have taken an innocent life and ruined my happiness. They deserve to be mobbed but the other way is better."[59]

Other Tulsans thought differently. Shortly before eleven o'clock on that same Saturday evening, several men in cars began to assemble in front of the courthouse. "In a few minutes," the *World* later reported, "the handful of men outside the building had increased to hundreds and shortly a thousand people blocked the streets in curiosity and anticipation." About fifty men in the crowd were armed with pistols and shotguns, and some had their faces covered with handkerchiefs. Soon, a delegation of these men entered the courthouse, and asked Sheriff Woolley for Belton. "Let the law take its course, boys," the sheriff was reported to have replied. "The electric chair will get him before long, but you know this is no way to interfere with the law." The men, however, were adamant, and they disarmed Woolley and ordered him to secure the release of Belton, who had been placed in a cell normally reserved for black prisoners on the top floor. Harmon and Sharp were left in their cells, and when Belton was led outside the courthouse, it was reported that onlookers cheered as his captors shouted, "We got him boys. We've got him."[60]

Belton's hands were bound, and he was placed inside Homer Nida's taxicab, which earlier had been stolen from the authorities. A large caravan of cars was formed, and after some zig-zagging through town, the line of cars, "nearly a mile long," drove to the spot near Red Fork where Nida had been shot. The city police arrived at the courthouse after Belton had been taken away, and according to Police Chief John Gustafson, "We did the best thing, jumped into cars and followed the ever increasing mob."[61]

Once at the desired spot, Belton's captors took him from the car and began to ask him why he had killed Nida. He denied that he had done so, and denied ever making a confession. The inquisition of Belton might have continued, but members of the crowd were anxious, and cries of "Where's the rope" and "Don't waste time" were to be heard. A rumor spread that a posse was in close pursuit, so the entire group moved to a spot along the Jenks road, about three miles southwest of Tulsa. By the time the crowd reassembled, it was reported that at least a thousand cars were present, and that women and children were among the onlookers. Most of the Tulsa police force had arrived, too, but they were instructed by Chief Gustafson not to intervene. Gustafson later justified his order by stating that "any demonstration from an officer would have started gun play and dozens of innocent people would have been killed and injured." Instead, the local police kept the onlookers from getting too close to Belton and his captors, and it has been reported that they also helped to direct traffic.[62]

Belton was led to the west side of the road, underneath a large signboard owned by the Federal Tire Company. A rope was secured from a nearby farmhouse, and a noose was thrown around his neck.

He asked for a cigarette, which he smoked as he silently stared at his captors. Roy Belton was then lynched.[63] His body hung for eleven minutes, during which time one of his executioners reportedly yelled: "Don't shoot! Don't anybody shoot! Let him hang and suffer like Nida suffered!"[64] The *World* later reported that "sudden pandemonium broke loose" when the body of Roy Belton dropped to the ground.

> Hundreds rushed over the prostrate form to get bits of the clothing. The rope was cut into bits for souvenirs. His trousers and shoes were torn into bits and the mob fairly fought over gruesome souvenirs.
>
> An ambulance was finally pushed through the jam of automobiles. The body was carried to the car, late arrivals still grabbing for bits of clothing on the now almost nude form.[65]

Belton's body was then taken back to an undertaker in the city, and it was reported that a crowd of several hundred people "gathered despite the late hour and insisted upon viewing the remains."[66]

Police Chief John Gustafson said later that the lynching, while "regrettable," was "probably inevitable because of the great feeling which had been aroused by the cruel manner in which Homer Nida was killed." Furthermore, he stated: "I do not condone mob law—in fact, I am absolutely opposed to it—but it is my honest opinion that the lynching of Belton will prove of real benefit to Tulsa and vicinity. It was an object lesson to the hijackers and auto thieves, and I believe it will be taken as such." Echoing the police chief, Sheriff Woolley stated that he thought the affair would prove beneficial to Tulsa because "it shows to the criminal that the men of Tulsa mean business." Tulsa Mayor T. D. Evans was out of town during the affair.[67]

The *World* called the event "a righteous protest" and stated: "There was not a vestige of the mob spirit in the act of Saturday night. It was citizenship, outraged by government inefficiency and a too tender regard to the professional criminal." The *Tribune* editorialized that "lynch law is never justified," but criticized the courts and "our high officials" rather than the lynchers of Roy Belton. The *World* also criticized government officials, including Sheriff Woolley. It reserved special venom, however, for Governor James B. Robertson, Acting Governor Waldrop, and Lieutenant Governor Trapp, all of whom publicly condemned the lynching. The

*World* accused them of having created a "pardoning orgy," and concluded that "it is not government we have here in Oklahoma but a
hideous travesty." Furthermore, the newspaper ominously stated,
"We predict that unless conditions are speedily improved," the
lynching of Belton "will not be the last by any means."[68]

Of Tulsa's three newspapers, only the *Star*, the city's black
weekly, announced itself as "unalterably opposed" to the event. The
editor of the *Star*, A. J. Smitherman, declared, "There is no crime,
however atrocious, that justifies mob violence." The black newspaper reported that, "sad to relate, Oklahoma shook hands with the
American lynching state of Georgia last Saturday night at Tulsa and
Sunday night at Oklahoma City by [the] lynching of a white boy and
a colored boy by mob violence." The *Star* added, prophetically: "The
lynching of Roy Belton explodes the theory that a prisoner is safe on
top of the Court House from mob violence."[69]

Chapter 3
# Race Riot

Roy Belton's death was of special significance to black Tulsans, whose brethren throughout the state were more and more the victims of white mobs. Any faith in the city's white law enforcement officials had been shattered by the events of 1920. If a white could be lynched in the "Magic City," what was to stop a mob from lynching a black? This question loomed large the next spring.

I

Opportunities for young black men in Tulsa in 1921 were severely circumscribed, regardless of education; therefore it is perhaps not very unusual that Dick Rowland had dropped out of Booker T. Washington High School to go to work downtown. One common occupation for Tulsa's teenage black males in the early 1920s was to work at the white-owned and white-patronized shoe shining parlors on Main Street. Robert Fairchild, who during his after-school hours worked with Rowland, recalled that these young people were paid five dollars a week. "But," he added, "the tips were just out of sight. At that time, you see, Tulsa was in the oil boom, and everybody would go to bed poor as Lazarus, and wake up rich as country butter. They didn't know what to do with their money, and they'd come down there and get a shine, and they'd give you a dollar as [soon as they'd give you] fifteen cents."[1]

There were no toilet facilities for the bootblacks, so the owner of

45

the shine parlor where Rowland worked arranged for his employees to use the restroom on the top floor of the nearby Drexel building. To get to the restroom, the bootblacks would have to ride up the elevator, which was operated by white women. So, as he often would do, on Monday morning, May 30, 1921, nineteen-year-old Dick Rowland went into the Drexel building to use the restroom. The elevator operator was a young white girl named Sarah Page, who was about seventeen years old. Minutes later, Dick Rowland ran out of the elevator. What actually transpired is probably forever clouded in obscurity, but many white Tulsans soon came to believe that Rowland had attacked the girl, scratched her hands, and tore her clothes.[2]

But there are many other accounts as to what happened, perhaps the most common being that Rowland accidentally stepped on Page's foot in the elevator, causing her to lurch back, and when he grabbed her arm to keep her from falling, she screamed.[3] In any event there is no real evidence that Dick Rowland attempted to assault Sarah Page. The preliminary police report on the incident did not mention Page by name, and the police did not arrest Rowland

Main Street, looking south from Third, in the early 1920s. The Drexel building is the fifth building down on the left. Across the street, barely visible beneath the Boston Shoe Store, is a sign for a shine parlor.

Courtesy of the McFarlin Library, University of Tulsa

until the next day. More importantly, those who knew Rowland at the time do not believe that he would have done such a thing, and as Walter White of the NAACP later wondered: why were so many people ready to believe that Rowland was so ignorant as to attempt a rape in a crowded office building within earshot of many people?[4]

Dick Rowland was arrested by two Tulsa police officers, one black and one white, on Tuesday. While the police were quietly conducting their investigation, the Tulsa *Tribune* decided to portray the incident in a vastly different light. What the Tuesday, May 31, 1921, issue of this newspaper said may never be known in its entirety. When the early issues of the *Tribune* were later microfilmed, someone had ripped out a front-page article and removed part of the editorial page. The original bound volumes of the newspaper have also been destroyed. However, in his 1946 thesis on the riot, Loren Gill stated that the *Tribune* "carried the following inflammatory news item prominently displayed on the front page":

The Drexel building.
Courtesy of the McFarlin Library, University of Tulsa

Nab Negro for Attacking
Girl in Elevator

A negro delivery boy who gave his name to the public as "Diamond Dick" but who has been identified as Dick Rowland, was arrested on South [sic] Greenwood avenue this morning by Officers Carmichael and Pack, charged with attempting to assault the 17-year-old white elevator girl in the Drexel building early yesterday.

He will be tried in municipal court this afternoon on a state charge.

The girl said she noticed the negro a few minutes before the attempted assault looking up and down the hallway on the third floor of the Drexel building as if to see if there was anyone in sight but thought nothing of it at the time.

A few minutes later he entered the elevator she claimed, and attacked her, scratching her hands and face and tearing her clothes. Her screams brought a clerk from Renberg's store to her assistance and the negro fled. He was captured and identified this morning both by the girl and the clerk, police say.

Tenants of the Drexel building said the girl is an orphan who works as an elevator operator to pay her way through business college.[5]

There can be but little doubt, however, that this issue of the *Tribune*, then edited by Richard Lloyd Jones, had more to say about the incident. Dr. P. S. Thompson, president of the Tulsa Medical, Dental, and Pharmaceutical Association, stated that the "immediate cause" of the riot "was a report in the Tulsa *Tribune* that threats were being made to lynch a Negro for attempted criminal assault upon a White girl, which was wholly without foundation or cause." One informant, W. D. Williams, has a vivid memory that the *Tribune* carried an article headlined, "To Lynch Negro Tonight."[6] Another person wrote after the riot that:

The Daily Tribune, a White newspaper that tries to gain its popularity by referring to the Negro settlement as "Little Africa," came out on the evening of Tuesday, May 31, with an article claiming that a Negro had had some trouble with a White elevator girl at the Drexel Bldg. It also said that a mob of whites were forming in order to lynch the Negro.[7]

Similarly, Adjutant General Charles Barrett, who led the National Guard into Tulsa to suppress the riot, stated that the riot had its origins in the Drexel building incident, and in "the fantastic write-up of the incident in a sensation-seeking newspaper."[8]

This issue of the *Tribune* hit the streets of Tulsa at about 3:15 P.M. Forty-five minutes later, a man called the police and notified them that there was lynch talk on the streets of the city, and Police and Fire Commissioner J. M. Adkison called Sheriff Willard McCullough and informed him of the same. The talk soon spread to action. Sometime between 6:00 and 7:00 P.M., a crowd of whites began to form outside of the courthouse, where Rowland was being held. It has been reported that there were some three hundred whites outside the courthouse by 7:30 P.M., and that this crowd grew to four hundred by nine o'clock.[9]

Sheriff McCullough later stated that when three white men walked into the courthouse around 8:20 P.M., he promptly ordered them out, telling them that there was not going to be a lynching. McCullough then went outside and ordered the crowd to disperse. However, he apparently did not attempt to enforce his order. The crowd of whites remained. Although the sheriff later claimed that he expected no serious trouble coming out of the situation, he did take some precautionary measures. He sent the elevator to the top floor of the building, where the jail was, and rendered it inoperable. He sent his guards to the top floor, too, where he had them barricade themselves behind a door at the top of the narrow and easily defendable flight of stairs. He ordered them not to open the door for anyone.[10]

Some black Tulsans were justly alarmed by these developments. The fate of Roy Belton after a similar crowd of whites had gathered outside of the courthouse less than a year before was a fresh memory. And there were enough recent incidents of blacks being spirited away from Oklahoma jails and lynched to give cause for alarm. With rightful urgency, black Tulsans gathered among themselves on Greenwood Avenue to discuss their options.[11]

Apparently, there was some confusion as to whether Sheriff McCullough desired and sought black aid for the defense of the courthouse. Barney Cleaver and another black policeman had been in touch with McCullough throughout the evening. Cleaver had called the sheriff and told him that there was a rumor circulating in the Greenwood business district that a white mob was forming. Cleaver asked if he could come down to the courthouse, but McCullough

Sheriff Willard McCullough.
Courtesy of the Tulsa *World*.

asked him to stay where he was and try to calm things down at that end. Later, the sheriff told Cleaver that he could come downtown. Other blacks stated that they had called McCullough to offer their assistance, and that he later requested it.[12]

At about 9:15 P.M., false reports reached the Greenwood area that the white mob was storming the courthouse. Henry Jacobs later stated that he saw J. B. Stratford, a hotel proprietor, getting together an armed group and telling some of his comrades: "Boys, we will send and get the Muskogee crowd and you go on up and lay there 'til they come." Another man claimed that he saw J. K. Smitherman, black deputy sheriff, go into a "choc" joint and collect some men to "go downtown" with him. Barney Cleaver stated that he tried to stop a group of blacks from going, but that they only laughed and threatened him. Some fifteen minutes later, a group of twenty-five to thirty black Tulsans armed with rifles and shotguns appeared at the courthouse and offered their services to Sheriff McCullough for the defense of the jail. Some police at the scene convinced these people that Rowland was safe, and that the authorities could handle any situation which might arise. Apparently reassured, the blacks left. The white crowd, however, remained.[13]

Rumors and reports of what was happening at the courthouse spread through the city. Action followed. Major James A. Bell of

Tulsa's National Guard units was informed at his home at about nine o'clock by two other guardsmen that a white lynch mob was forming outside of the courthouse. Bell then went to the National Guard armory and called Sheriff McCullough and Police Chief John Gustafson about the situation, and reportedly, they both informed him that matters were under control. Nevertheless, as a precautionary measure, Bell told the Guard officers at the armory to gather together all the arms and ammunition, and to start contacting the other guardsmen in case Governor Robertson called them out.[14]

Major Bell then returned to his home to put on his uniform, but when he got there two runners informed him that a mob of whites was trying to break into the armory. Bell grabbed his pistol and returned to the armory, where he first spotted a group of white men trying to force a window on the side of the building. He ordered them away, and followed them to the front of the armory, where some three to four hundred whites had gathered. The crowd demanded rifles and ammunition. Bell refused. He later stated that they "continued to press forward in a threatening manner," and that only by maintaining a firm stand with pistols drawn were he and a few others able to keep the crowd from entering the building. Bell told the crowd that the guardsmen inside would shoot any unauthorized visitors. The mob was finally dispersed, and Bell threw guards around the building.[15]

Undoubtedly spurred on by more reports and by the growth of the white crowd in front of the courthouse—now consisting of 1,500 to 2,000 people—armed blacks visited the courthouse for a second time. It was approximately 10:30 P.M. They numbered, this time, between fifty and seventy-five men. Again they offered their services to the police, who were dwarfed by the white crowd, and again they were refused and asked to leave. By this time, Barney Cleaver had arrived and was trying to convince his fellow black Tulsans to go back home. Sheriff McCullough later stated that he disarmed one black man by himself, but did not order his deputies to conduct a general disarmament because he feared that this would start a riot. He stated that he wanted to get the blacks in a frame of mind to leave. Apparently, however, neither the sheriff nor Chief Gustafson had seriously attempted to disperse the crowd of whites or get them

Barney Cleaver, Tulsa's first black
police officer.

to leave, and there is evidence to suggest that Gustafson had not even called the entire police force to the scene. In any event, not all of Tulsa's police were there.[16]

Purportedly, the blacks were in the process of leaving when a white man approached one of their number. According to the version heard by Robert Fairchild, the white approached a tall black veteran who was carrying an Army issue 45-caliber and said, "Nigger, what are you doing with that pistol?"

"I'm going to use it if I need to," came the reply.

"No, you give it to me."

"Like hell I will."

The white man then attempted to disarm the veteran and a shot was fired. Sheriff McCullough stated that from that moment "the race war was on and I was powerless to stop it." Black and white Tulsans exchanged gunfire, and Walter White of the NAACP reported that a dozen people fell in this initial gunplay. Numerically overwhelmed by the whites, the blacks began to retreat toward Greenwood. After the battle had swung out of the range of the courthouse, white doctors and ambulance crews tried to assist a wounded black man who was lying on the sidewalk. But white crowd members would not allow them to aid him, and "he lay writhing on the sidewalk, under a billboard from which smiled winsomely the face of Mary Pickford, America's sweetheart."[17]

## II

Reports of what was happening in Tulsa began to filter in to the state authorities in Oklahoma City as the evening wore on. Major Byron Kirkpatrick of the Tulsa National Guard units called Adjutant General Charles F. Barrett, who commanded Oklahoma's National Guard, and told him that the situation was looking grim even before violence broke out at the courthouse. Governor James B. A. Robertson was informed by Tulsa Police Chief John Gustafson at 10:30 that the authorities in Tulsa could manage the situation. Chief Gustafson's message to the governor was somewhat odd, because a half an hour earlier he had asked Major Bell if the Tulsa guardsmen could be used to assist the local authorities, but was informed by Bell that he would need an official order for this.[18] The city broke out into open warfare within minutes after this call.

After talking with Gustafson, Bell, and Robertson, Adjutant General Barrett ordered the mobilization of the Tulsa National Guard units. They were ordered to give the civil authorities in Tulsa any assistance necessary. Governor Robertson, however, felt that more action was needed, and since the Tulsa authorities were apparently content with matters as they stood, he took the initiative. Shortly after midnight, he ordered Major Kirkpatrick in Tulsa to draw up a telegram—addressed to the governor—requesting that the National Guard be sent into the city. He then ordered Kirkpatrick to get Gustafson, McCullough, and any district judge he could find to sign it, since at that time Oklahoma law required that a request for the National Guard to be sent into any area needed the signatures of the local police chief, the county sheriff, and a local judge. Kirkpatrick secured the signatures of Gustafson and Judge Valjean Biddison apparently with little difficulty, but had some trouble getting that of McCullough, as the sheriff was barricaded with some of his men— and Dick Rowland—inside the courthouse. Eventually, however, he completed his task, and by 3:00 A.M., June 1, the orders for the mobilization of National Guard troops in Oklahoma City to be sent to Tulsa had been announced.[19]

Meanwhile, Tulsa had been the scene of various "mobilization" activities, too. After the initial fighting had moved away from the courthouse, the Tulsa police deputized scores of whites—many of whom had been part of the crowd in front of the courthouse. At a meeting held by these "special deputies" a very light-skinned black Tulsan, who could "pass" for white learned that they planned to invade the Greenwood district from the west. He then returned to black Tulsa and told his roommate, Seymour Williams, what he had learned. Williams, an Army veteran who had been wounded in France, who was then a teacher at the Booker T. Washington School, went home and got his Army revolver. He then went down to Greenwood Avenue, which was a scene of commotion, and spread the word. But, he recalled, "not a damn one" would come along with him, and he spent the entire night guarding an intersection that his roommate had told him was to be a key invasion spot for the whites. Although Williams did not stem the invasion into black Tulsa, the information proved to be correct, as the spot was visited several times by whites, including a policeman.[20]

Shortly before 11:00 P.M., the order for the mobilization of the Tulsa National Guard units was received, and two Guard officers took some of the local guardsmen whom they had assembled down to the police station. At some point along the way, they received a report that a group of whites had broken into McGee's Hardware Store, stealing guns and ammunition. The owner of the store, however, later stated that he thought that Captain George H. Blaine of the Tulsa police force was the one who broke into his store and dealt out the guns. The guardsmen finally arrived at the store, which was located directly across from the police station, removed what was left of the crowd of whites, and locked it up. McGee's store was not the only one broken into by whites in their search for weapons, as fifteen other hardware stores and pawnshops reported break-ins on the night of May 31, and some $42,923 worth of merchandise was stolen.[21]

There was still a crowd of whites in front of the courthouse when

Police Inspector C. W. Daley arrived there at midnight from out of town. The attention of the whites, however, was no longer focused entirely on Dick Rowland, but had come to include most of Tulsa's black citizenry. These first few hours of the riot, from its inception until around 1:00 A.M. (June 1), were primarily marked by preparation: any whites who had been without guns now secured them. Some blacks prepared for a possible onslaught, while some may have left town. Some Tulsans, of course, were unaware of what was happening. Many blacks in this category, however, soon learned, as the initial period was not without its violence. The slow, retreating battle which some blacks were fighting with the whites soon approached black Tulsa's doorstep.[22]

The first fire broke out at about 1:00 A.M. at the intersection of Archer Street and Boston Avenue along the fringe of the black district. The fire department arrived at the scene, but a mob of some five hundred whites prevented the firemen from working and soon forced them to return with their equipment to the station. By this time the battle had begun to encroach upon black Tulsa, and armed blacks were now in their home territory. Occasionally, a car full of armed whites roared down the street in a black neighborhood, guns blazing indiscriminately. White rioters attempting to cross the railyard and invade the black district had to contend with the gunfire of black residents defending their property. Black Tulsans were outnumbered, but had the advantage of being in defensive positions on well-known ground. Probably the most active fighting that night occurred along the Frisco Railroad tracks, located between First and Archer streets, which formed an important boundary between black and white Tulsa.[23]

About the hour of daybreak—4:30 A.M.—Police Inspector Daley arrived at the Frisco Railroad station, where he found that the guards he had previously posted there were engulfed by a mob of whites preparing to enter the black district. Daley drew his pistol and threatened to shoot any member of the crowd who tried to advance. He instructed a friend to call the police station for assistance, but was informed that all of the police were either in the hills outside of town, or out rounding up and interning blacks. The combination of Daley and the armed black residents of the area managed to hold

White rioters breaking into the home of a well-to-do black
Tulsan . . .

. . . and setting it on fire.

back this Frisco station crowd for about one and a half hours. But around 6:00 A.M. they rushed past Daley en masse and invaded black Tulsa.[24]

In these early morning hours of June 1, 1921, the wholesale burning and looting of black Tulsa began. Fighting continued, but black defenders were hampered by the fact that they were greatly outnumbered, and because the police were either nowhere to be found or were busy disarming and interning *black* Tulsans. Some of the fires in the Greenwood business district were probably started just prior to the mass invasion of the whites. O. W. Gurley stated that "early in the morning" he looked out of a window of his three-story brick hotel and saw a few white men in khaki clothing set fire to it and other brick buildings along Greenwood Avenue. Upon seeing this, he and his wife ran from their hotel. A black man running ahead of them was gunned down by whites. Mrs. Gurley then fell and her husband, thinking she was dead, ran on alone a few blocks to the Dunbar School. Hidden in the basement, Gurley reported seeing over one thousand white people pass by on the street. They set fire to the school, but he stayed in it until the roof caved in. "Then I thought it was death to stay and death to go," Gurley said, "but I finally crawled out and was taken to the ball park by a white gentleman."[25]

Initially, much of the looting and burning by the whites centered upon the southernmost sections of black Tulsa, which included its business district and some of its poorer neighborhoods. At around 6:40 A.M., fires were started in the shanties along Archer Street, and one hour later, both sides of Archer from Boston to Elgin streets were burning. "Deep Greenwood" was soon looted and put to the torch. The Mt. Zion Baptist Church, an impressive structure which had only recently been built, was burned by white Tulsans after a gun battle took place outside of it. One elderly black woman sat in front of her home on Latimer Street and refused to leave when a group of whites came. She told them that they would burn her house if she left, and if they were going to do that, they might as well kill her then and there. She stayed, and lived, and her house was not burned. There is also evidence that white owners of structures in black areas stood in front of them to ward off the rioters' torch.[26]

White rioter and the burning homes of black Tulsans.

Church members rush to save the furnishings of the Mt. Zion Baptist Church. White Tulsans later tried to justify their destruction of the newly built church by circulating false reports that it contained an "arsenal."

White rioters and onlookers were given a free reign of the city's streets while the predominantly white police force occupied its time imprisoning black citizens.

There were many atrocities. An elderly black couple was murdered on their way home from church. Dr. A. C. Jackson, named by the Mayo brothers as "the most able Negro surgeon in America," was murdered by whites after he had surrendered to one group of whites who had promised him protection, and were escorting him to Convention Hall for internment. A white man was mistaken for a black by a group of whites and was summarily killed. A white woman was shot on the porch of her home at about 7:30 A.M. One black was murdered in front of Convention Hall after he had surrendered. At one point, an incoming passenger train, unaware of the situation in Tulsa, arrived on one of the railway lines where heavy fighting was in progress. No one on the train was injured, but its windows were shattered by bullets.[27]

In spite of the fires, white rioters could still be found in black areas off Archer at 9:00 A.M. Many black Tulsans, rounded up at random by the police, were being taken prisoner by this time. Many were forcibly removed from their homes by the police, by National Guardsmen, by numerous "special deputies," and by various unauthorized whites. Some of these "arrests" were made by white women. Although some whites drove blacks around downtown in vehicles, the majority of the prisoners were taken to three improvised internment centers: Convention Hall, McNulty [baseball] Park, and the fairgrounds. All of these actions, needless to say, rendered the defense of black property impossible. In general, police actions played right into the hands of the white rioters who were looting and burning. The internment process did not occur without black opposition, but again, black Tulsans were simply outnumbered.[28]

Efforts by some whites to limit the destructiveness of the riot failed. As the white rioters moved further north, they entered more of black Tulsa's residential districts. At 9:30 A.M., John P. Richards, the white principal of the Sequoyah School, called the police about the stretch of black homes along part of North Detroit Avenue, perhaps black Tulsa's wealthiest neighborhood. He told the police that this area was still untouched by violence, and that a few police officers—if dispatched immediately—could protect this area from destruction. Richards stated that the police said they would send a few

Calm amid the storm.
Courtesy of the Metropolitan Tulsa Chamber of Commerce

Black Tulsa engulfed by flames, June 1, 1921. A northerly view looking toward "Deep Greenwood" from across the Frisco railyards.
Courtesy of the McFarlin Library, University of Tulsa

The destruction of June 1, seen from probably the northeast, with either the Santa Fe or Midland Valley tracks in the foreground.
Courtesy of the Metropolitan Tulsa Chamber of Commerce

Looking west toward Greenwood. The Red Cross estimated that over one thousand homes were burned by the white rioters.
Courtesy of the McFarlin Library, University of Tulsa

men, but they never came. Shortly after his call, a group of whites came to the area, looted, and set fire to each of these homes.[29]

### III

Adjutant General Barrett and the National Guard troops from Oklahoma City arrived in Tulsa by train at about 9:15 A.M. By that time, much of the gunplay between blacks and whites had died down, though looting continued. Black Tulsa was burning. For many black citizens, there was literally no place to hide. Some fled the city and received rough treatment at the hands of whites in some of the smaller towns outside of Tulsa. Some white vigilantes even roamed affluent white neighborhoods to round up black live-in domestic workers. One carload of whites dragged a black corpse around the streets of downtown. And in the downtown area, as well as in some of the white neighborhoods, trucks loaded with corpses were observed by some residents. Sheriff McCullough slipped out of town with Dick Rowland at about eight o'clock.[30]

When the National Guardsmen arrived, they did not immediately take to the streets. Barrett went to City Hall and set up his headquarters, while his troops prepared and ate breakfast. In light of the disorder in Tulsa, Barrett called Governor Robertson and requested that he decree martial law throughout the city. Robertson agreed, and martial law was declared at 11:29 A.M. Barrett had circulars announcing the decree posted throughout the city.[31]

Once activated, the guardsmen concentrated their efforts on aiding the fire department in their renewed efforts to control the city's fires. They also began to imprison any black Tulsans who had not yet been interned. The guards took imprisoned blacks out of the hands of the "special deputies" and other groups of whites. Barrett ordered Mayor Evans to revoke all of these special commissions, which Evans did, claiming that many of the men who held them were the mob leaders themselves.[32]

Throughout the day, many blacks were taken to the fairgrounds, as Convention Hall was full. Apparently some whites were also taken to this site, which was guarded by thirteen National Guardsmen. Whites were disarmed by guardsmen throughout the city, but were generally merely sent home. Sixty-five whites, however, were

Armed whites searching blacks.

Courtesy of the McFarlin Library, University of Tulsa

En route to an internment center. Tulsa physician A. C. Jackson, who had been named by the Mayo brothers as "the most able Negro surgeon in America," was murdered on one such march.

Courtesy of the Metropolitan Tulsa Chamber of Commerce

Whites collecting black prisoners.

Courtesy of the Metropolitan Tulsa Chamber of Commerce

arrested by the troops, and a truckload of rifles was seized from one group of whites.[33]

As is the case with many aspects of the riot, there is some confusion over the use of airplanes. During the violence, police took over private airplanes and flew over the city. After the riot, planes were sent out to observe any unusual activity in virtually every substantial black community in northeastern Oklahoma, purportedly because many white Tulsans feared a black counterattack. There is other evidence, however, on the subject of airplanes. Mary E. Jones Parrish, a black Tulsan who experienced the riot, passionately described those early morning hours:

> After watching the men unload on First Street where we could see them from our windows, we heard such a buzzing noise that on running to the door to get a better view of what was going on, the sights our eyes beheld made our poor hearts stand still for a moment. There was a great shadow in the sky and upon a second look we discerned that this cloud was caused by fast approaching enemy aeroplanes. It then dawned upon us that the enemy had organized in the night and was invading our district the same as the Germans invaded France and Belgium. The firing of guns was renewed in quick succession. People were seen to flee from their burning homes, some with babes in their arms and leading crying and excited children by the hand; others, old and feeble, all fleeing to safety. Yet, seemingly, I could not leave. I walked as one in a horrible dream. By this time my little girl was up and dressed, but I made her lie on the dufold in order that bullets must penetrate it before reaching her. By this time a machine gun had been installed in the granary and was raining bullets down on our section.

Parrish's account only implies that planes may have attacked the area, but the Chicago *Defender* reported directly that black neighborhoods in Tulsa were bombed from the air by a private plane equipped with dynamite.[34]

After martial law was declared, violence generally ceased and some relief work began. The Tulsa race riot, one of the most devastating single incidents of racial violence in twentieth century America, was over within twenty-four hours of its inception. While most rioters returned to their homes, most of Tulsa's black citizenry was imprisoned; over six thousand blacks were reported as being interned on the night of June 1. Others had fled the city. Upward of

At first, some blacks were taken downtown.

Courtesy of the McFarlin Library, University of Tulsa

Pride and defiance in the midst of catastrophe.

Courtesy of the McFarlin Library, University of Tulsa

Even the children were guarded.

Courtesy of the McFarlin Library, University of Tulsa

The internment process at Convention Hall. At least one black was killed here by whites.

fifty people—both blacks and whites—were dead. Over one thousand homes and businesses—much of black Tulsa—lay in ruin, a smoldering monument to crushed dreams.[35]

IV

The total number of people who died in the Tulsa race riot of 1921 is very much in question; estimates range from 27 to over 250. The estimates themselves fall into three major groups: the first counts around thirty deaths; the second, which is probably the most accurate, sets the figure at around seventy-five; the last places the number at one hundred and seventy-five and above.

Newspaper estimates were at first generally rather high, but took a plunge during the first week after the riot. The Tulsa *Tribune* of June 1, 1921, gave two sets of figures. In a story on the riot, it reported that 9 whites and 68 blacks had died. But a bulletin in that same issue stated that some 175 people were known dead. The next day, the *Tribune* reported that it knew for sure of only 31 deaths: 9 whites and 22 blacks. The New York *Times* of June 2, 1921, reported that 9 whites and 68 blacks were known to have died in the riot. Six days later, the newspaper reported that only 33 people had been killed.[36]

Judging from the large number of people who were reported wounded and the steps which the authorities took in regard to them, it seems that the death toll was most likely toward the higher estimates. On the morning of June 1 the National Guard turned the armory into a makeshift hospital for wounded blacks. On that same day, Major Paul R. Brown was placed in charge of the medical and surgical situation in the city. Under his guidance, guardsmen took over a rooming house which had once been the Cinnabar Hospital, and reconverted it—with the aid of the Red Cross—into a hospital for seriously wounded black Tulsans. A house in North Tulsa was taken over for the walking wounded. The National Guard also took charge of six beds in the Oklahoma Hospital, and another six in the Tulsa Hospital, for black women.[37]

Red Cross records reflect a sizeable amount of physical suffering. Its records included the names of 48 whites who passed through hospitals after the riot. The director of Red Cross operations, Maurice

Willows, however, believed the number to be higher. It has been suggested that many whites would not give their names when they were treated for wounds for fear of later being subjected to legal actions against them. Red Cross materials also revealed that 183 blacks were given surgical treatment within twenty-four hours after the riot, with over 70 percent of these people being hospitalized. The organization gave first aid treatment to some 531 persons, and during the first week after the riot, about twenty doctors (eleven of whom were black) performed some 163 operations, 82 of them classified as "major" operations.[38]

The black sick and wounded—those who were attended to—were initially taken to six private hospitals in addition to the newly reconverted Cinnabar Hospital. Shortly after the violence, four large hospital wards were constructed in the Booker T. Washington School— which had escaped destruction by the white rioters—and many black patients had been transferred there within two weeks.[39]

The Red Cross cared for some black patients until the end of September, 1921. Exactly how much service was rendered by the city's private hospitals is somewhat unclear. On July 26, 1921, Dr. Fred S. Clinton of the Oklahoma Hospital filed a claim against the Tulsa Police Department in the sum of $3,900 for hospital, medical, and surgical service rendered to it ($3,381.10 was eventually paid). On September 23, 1921, the Tulsa County Commissioners communicated to the City Commission that it was prepared to turn over any hospital equipment which it had any interest in to the Frissel Hospital, apparently in response to riot services.[40]

Another complication in estimating the number of riot fatalities is a consequence of the action taken by Adjutant General Barrett on June 2, 1921. Barrett banned all funerals from taking place in the city, citing as his reasons military policy, the emotional stress which still prevailed, and the fact that many churches, he claimed, were being used to shelter the homeless.[41] If funerals were against the expressed policy of the military authorities, then what happened to the riot dead? How were they buried? There is some evidence regarding these issues, some of which is contradictory. In his magazine article on the riot, "The Eruption of Tulsa," Walter White stated:

Victim.
Courtesy of the Metropolitan Tulsa Chamber of Commerce

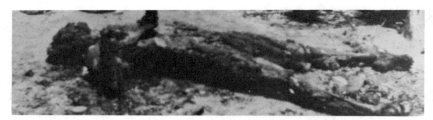

Metal bedsteads: ghostly sentinels of Tulsa's black residential neighborhoods.
Courtesy of the Metropolitan Tulsa Chamber of Commerce

Victim. Walter White, of the NAACP, reported: "One story was told to me by an eyewitness of five colored men trapped in a burning house. Four were burned to death. A fifth attempted to flee, was shot to death as he emerged from the burning structure, and his body was thrown back into the flames."
Courtesy of the Metropolitan Tulsa Chamber of Commerce

Smoldering dreams.
Courtesy of the Metropolitan Tulsa Chamber of Commerce

O. T. Johnson, Commandant of the Tulsa Citadel of the Salvation Army, stated that on Wednesday and Thursday, the Salvation Army fed thirty-seven Negroes employed as grave diggers, and twenty on Friday and Saturday. During the first two days these men dug 120 graves in each of which a dead Negro was buried. No coffins were used. The bodies were dumped into the holes and covered with dirt. Added to the number accounted for were numbers of others—men, women and children—who were incinerated in the burning houses in the Negro settlement. One story was told to me by an eye-witness of five colored men trapped in a burning house. Four burned to death. A fifth attempted to flee, was shot to death as he emerged from the burning structure, and his body was thrown back into the flames.[42]

Ross T. Warner and Henry Whitlow have stated that they saw corpses piled onto trucks which were driven away. Warner stated that he saw at least thirty dead blacks transported in that fashion. It has also been reported by some that dead bodies were dumped into the Arkansas River. Certain city officials and physicians, however, stated in the 1940s that "all those who were killed were given decent burials."[43]

Furthermore, it should be noted that the estimates of official and semi-official groups of the riot fatalities do not necessarily agree. The estimate of the Department of Health's Bureau of Vital Statistics was that 10 whites and 26 blacks had died in the violence. Estimates *in* Red Cross records—not necessarily its own estimate—on the other hand, ran as high as 300 deaths.[44]

Finally, it should be noted that not everyone has agreed that more blacks died in the race riot than whites. W. D. Williams has disputed this assumption, citing as evidence the large number of whites which he saw get shot by black snipers as they attempted to invade "Deep Greenwood." The Oklahoma City *Black Dispatch* of June 10, 1921, reported that it had received a letter from "a prominent Negro in the city of Tulsa" who stated that "from what he could learn on the ground, about one hundred were killed, equally divided between the two races."[45]

The amount of property lost due to the riot is likewise an elusive quantity. The most common estimate for the amount of real property lost was originally the estimate of the Tulsa Real Estate Exchange. It estimated the loss at about $1.5 million, one third of the total being in the (black) business district. The Exchange also estimated personal property loss at about $750,000. When considering these estimates, however, it is important to recall that the Exchange temporarily approved the designs of the City Commission and others to relocate part of Tulsa's black community and to use that land for a new train station. Estimates in Red Cross records revealed that 1,115 residences had been destroyed during the riot, and that another 314 houses were looted but not burned. The Tulsa *World* reported that some 338 people suffered losses of real estate, 82 of whom were black.[46]

Another source of evidence for property loss are the claims which were filed against the City of Tulsa for losses due to the riot. The minutes of the Tulsa City Commission meetings from June 14, 1921, to June 6, 1922, reveal that in excess of $1.8 million in claims against the city were filed with—and subsequently disallowed by—the city commissioners.[47] It has also been stated that by July 30, 1921, more than 1,400 law suits for losses upward of $4 million had been filed.[48] The claims filed against the city ranged from under $25 to over $150,000. Emma Gurley, a black woman whose family owned the Gurley Hotel (the Gurley building), filed a claim for its loss in excess of $150,000. Loula T. Williams filed a claim for over $100,000 for the destruction of the Dreamland Theatre and the Williams building. R. G. Dunn and Company reportedly lost some $250,000 in goods. Other large losses included the newly constructed Mount Zion Baptist Church (reportedly built at a cost of $85,000), and the offices of both of Tulsa's black newspapers, the Tulsa *Star* and the Oklahoma *Sun*.[49]

The results of the various surveys which were taken by the Red Cross are yet another source of information of the volume of property destruction. As ambiguous as the results were, they reported that one week after the riot, some 5,366 persons had been, to quote Loren L. Gill, "more or less seriously affected by the riot."[50]

Chapter 4
# Law, Order, and the Politics of Relief

I

The aftermath of the riot provides us with a valuable view of the interworkings of power, race relations, and racial ideologies in Tulsa. The various responses to the riot revealed both humanitarianism and greed, mutual aid and exploitation. "Relief" efforts were in some cases honest, while in many others were but a guise for further abuse. The characters were many.

The first problem faced by black Tulsans after the riot was a question of getting free. Roughly one-half of the city's black population was forcibly interned under armed guards—at Convention Hall, in public buildings downtown, at the baseball park, and at the fairgrounds. James T. West, a teacher at the Booker T. Washington School, reported that "people were herded in like cattle" into the Convention Hall, and that "the sick and wounded were dumped in front of the building and remained without attention for hours." At least one black man was shot in front of this large auditorium on Brady Street. Other blacks had a grand tour of imprisonment. Although he was interned at Convention Hall first, Jack Thomas was taken to a Catholic Church, then to the fairgrounds, and finally to a Methodist Church. By June 2, all black Tulsans who were interned—over 4,000—had been moved to the fairgrounds.[1]

There, they were held under armed sentries and "sheltered" in the cattle and hog pens. Food, clothing, and some bedding were given out on June 1 and 2. Apparently the physical condition of the prisoners generated concern among doctors, as vaccinations for smallpox, tetanus, and typhoid were administered to some 1,800 people at the camp during its first few days of existence. Black men did road repair work around the camp under the direction of the National Guard.[2]

At first, black Tulsans were allowed to leave the camp only if a white person would come and vouch for them, a system designed to allow only those blacks who were employed by whites to be released immediately. Generally, any white employer could secure the release of a black employee by identifying that person and promising that he or she would be kept "indoors or at the scene of their labor." There were, of course, some exceptions. J. C. Latimer, a black architect and contractor who was interned, claimed that he did not know any whites since he was self-employed. He later stated that a white man lied to the authorities and claimed him as his brother-in-law to gain his release. A few black Tulsans such as Dr. R. T. Bridgewater, an assistant county physician whose home had been burned by whites, worked outside of the camp during the day and returned to it at night to sleep for at least a short period. Most of the imprisoned citizens, once they secured their release, left for good. The 4,000 plus of June 2 dwindled to 450 by June 7. Eight days later, the fairgrounds were empty.[3]

In addition to the internment camps, black Tulsans faced other restrictions. While on the streets, they were required to wear or carry a green card with the words "Police Protection" printed on one side, and various other data recorded on the other, including the person's name, address, and employer. It has been reported that "any black found on the street without a green card properly filled out was arrested and sent back to the detention camp." Black Tulsans had to carry these cards, which had been paid for by the City Commission and the Chamber of Commerce, until July 7.[4]

Blacks were not allowed to purchase or possess firearms for a period of several weeks. On June 6 an order was issued which prohibited the use of servants' quarters in white districts by blacks "other than those employed regularly on the premises" prior to the riot.

Internment at McNulty baseball park.
Courtesy of the McFarlin Library, University of Tulsa

White Tulsans roamed the streets while blacks were imprisoned.
Courtesy of the McFarlin Library, University of Tulsa

Greenwood Avenue, looking north from Archer.
Courtesy of Western History Collections, University of Oklahoma Library

Theodore Baugham, black editor of the *Oklahoma Sun*, "succeeded in getting out a little daily paper," which included lists of people trying to locate their loved ones. However, it is highly doubtful that Baugham was in complete control of the editorial policy of this paper. The June 7 report of the Chamber of Commerce's Executive Welfare Committee reported that "a negro publication resumed to quiet the negroes," and Chamber records showed a receipt for a bill to pay for a paper which was "used as a medium to keep the negroes in form [*sic*] during the few days immediately following the riot." Baugham's *Oklahoma Sun* and A. J. Smitherman's Tulsa *Star*—both of whose offices were destroyed by the white rioters—were blamed by whites for causing the riot.[5]

The Red Cross estimated that at least 715 black families left Tulsa but returned later for "various reasons." On June 2, the New York *Times* reported a statement by members of a railroad crew that they passed some three thousand blacks heading north from Tulsa to Bartlesville—undoubtedly an exaggerated report. Some two hundred Tulsans left the city by rail, perhaps permanently, during the first two weeks after the riot. One hundred and fifty of these had their tickets purchased by the Red Cross. The others, who could purchase their own tickets, were charged only half fare. But not all black Tulsans who wanted to leave, even temporarily, were able to do so. Police, guardsmen, and "relief" workers combed areas north and east of town and took many of the people whom they found there to the internment centers.[6]

## II

Tulsa's first experience under martial law was brief. Business hours in the city were initially set from 8 A.M. to 6 P.M., except for groceries, meat markets, and other agencies contributing to the "comfort of the people." No automobiles, except for those of physicians, the Red Cross, or the police, were allowed on the street during the night. The National Guard authorities further deemed that any persons who were found on the streets with arms without "written permission from military authority or by virtue of proper commission under civil law, will be considered as public enemies and treated accordingly." The troops stood guard at various points throughout the city.[7]

Life under martial law was modified on June 2 and 3, and then terminated on the latter date. The modifications were enacted through a number of "field orders" issued by Adjutant General Barrett. Field Order No. 1 altered military rule so as to allow the civil authorities to begin prosecution of alleged rioters. The second did a number of things. It allowed most normal business and social activities to resume (at least for whites), and it removed all guardsmen from the "business area," which presumably referred to the "white" business area, namely downtown. However, the field order also decreed that people would be allowed neither "to congregate on the streets nor engage in heated controversy." It forbade any white people from going into the burned black district without a pass from the military. Blacks were to be allowed in the "burnt district or negro quarters" if they presented their "police protection" cards. This field order further declared that "all negroes living outside of the city and now detained in the various refugee and detention places will be held under detention and brought before the authorities at the city hall for investigation."[8]

Field Order No. 3 prohibited funerals in the city. The fourth order dealt particularly with the city's interned black population. In essence, it enacted forced labor:

> All the able-bodied negro men remaining in detention camp at the Fair Grounds and other places in the city of Tulsa will be required to render such service and perform such labor as is required by the military commission and the Red Cross in making the sanitary provisions for the care of the refugees.
>
> Able-bodied women not having the care of children, will also be required to perform such service as may be required in the feeding and care of refugees.
>
> This order covers any labor necessary in the care of the health or welfare of those people, by reason of their misfortune, must be looked after by different agencies of relief.[9]

Adjutant General Barrett also directed the county registrar to stop registering deeds from the destroyed area.[10]

The termination of martial law did not, however, produce an immediate end of the military's presence in the city. The Tulsa units of the National Guard remained on active duty until the morning of June 4, at which time some of them were to leave for their annual summer encampment. Battery "B" of the Tulsa-based 2nd Field Artillery was to remain in the city, "held in readiness" to cooperate with city and county authorities if needed, but was not to act as an organization unless ordered to do so by the governor.[11]

When it was announced on June 2 that martial law was to be ended in Tulsa the next day, some people were disturbed. During a directors' meeting of the Chamber of Commerce on June 3, "a motion prevailed appointing a committee . . . to confer with the general executive welfare committee and ask that martial law and the troops be maintained in Tulsa for at least one more week." One member of this newly appointed committee was the Reverend Harold G. Cooke, the white pastor of the Centenary Methodist Church, who stated three days later that blacks were the most at blame for the riot. He further claimed that there had been "no spirit of mob violence" amongst the crowd of whites in front of the courthouse, which included him, "but when criminal and liquor-frenzied niggers appeared on the streets and outraged the white people of this community, the thing was off."[12]

It is also possible that some black Tulsans may have desired that the National Guard troops, at least those sent in from the state capital, remain in the city for a longer period. After the riot, Mary E. Jones Parrish performed interviews for the Inter-Racial Commission, and of them she stated, "everyone with whom I met was loud in praise of the State troops who so gallantly came to the rescue of stricken Tulsa." But in reference to the "Home Guards"—by which she probably was referring to the numerous "special deputies"—she found denunciation of them "on every lip." This attitude was echoed by E. A. Loupe, a black plumber, who claimed that the "Home Guards" had offered no protection to blacks during the riot, but "joined in with the hoodlums in shooting in good citizens' homes." Seeing this, Loupe took his family and a few friends in his automobile and drove four miles outside the city, "where we were

This white couple apparently thought that the destruction in "Deep Greenwood" might make a good backdrop for a snapshot. They were not alone in a desire to commemorate the riot, for later one group of white entrepreneurs sold postcards of photographs of the riot and its aftermath, including photos of corpses.

Courtesy of Western History Collections, University of Oklahoma Library

The brick shells of the black business district loom behind the remains of black homes in the foreground.

Courtesy of Western History Collections, University of Oklahoma Library

gathered up by the State troops who were perfect gentlemen and treated us like citizens of real America."[13]

To replace the departed guardsmen, American Legion members were sworn in as police officers and "a force of 100 emergency minute men" was organized by Colonel P. J. Hurley in conjunction with the sheriff's office and the Chamber of Commerce. This group of "minute men" was better known as the Business Men's Protective League, and it played an active role in the "policing" of the city. Its members guarded the roads leading into Tulsa under instructions to halt any suspicious looking persons or automobiles, using force if necessary. In at least one instance, these guards did shoot, severely wounding a man and slightly injuring his sister when they refused a command to stop their car.[14]

This guarding of the highways leading into the city was a response to the lingering fear that many white Tulsans had of a black "counterattack" from outlying areas. Captain Blaine of the Tulsa police made a "scouting trip" by airplane to several centers of the black population in eastern Oklahoma to investigate rumors that blacks were preparing for some form of retaliatory violence. He found no such evidence. Perhaps the first rumor of this kind occurred on June 1, when Colonel Rooney of the National Guard heard that some five hundred black Muskogeeans were en route to Tulsa by train. He enacted precautionary measures to meet the train, but the report proved false. These rumors, and the actions which they generated, also tended to increase the isolation from the outside world which black Tulsa found itself in after the riot. For the first few days after the violence, all blacks who came to Tulsa from other communities were turned away at the city limits by white guards unless they agreed to take a black person home with them. One further example of the fear that there was more violence to come, or that violence in Tulsa could easily be provoked, was the fact that for several days after the riot the Pullman Company would not allow black porters to work on trains passing through Tulsa.[15]

### III

The restoration of law and order was the first priority in post-riot Tulsa, and the military authorities played the key role in this undertaking. Other needs, however, such as relief for the victims of the riot, were nearly as urgent. But here, as in most other post-riot activities, the primary players were civilians.

Any grass-roots actions of charity by Tulsa's white citizenry were generally limited to the first few days after the riot. On the morning of June 1, white citizens and church groups, in addition to the Salvation Army, "brought in coffee and sandwiches for the men on duty and prisoners and refugees." The Chamber of Commerce reported that on June 7 "dozens" of automobiles had been consigned to the Red Cross, and that "thousands of articles of wearing apparel and household utensils were assembled and distributed to the needy." Much of this activity was probably organized by the white churches and service groups, but one student of the riot has written that by June 3 "there was little activity at any of the churches except that they were used as collection points for bedding and clothing." Perhaps of questionable altruism, and an example which helps to illuminate the dubious nature of much of the local white "relief" activities, was the donation of fifty pieces of luggage by a Tulsa trunk company for use by homeless black Tulsans.[16]

Yet, regardless of the general lack of sympathy in white Tulsa for the conditions faced by their black brethren, and the extremely minimal and brief charitable activities which the local whites performed, "honest" relief work did continue in Tulsa, primarily through the Red Cross and the "Colored Citizens Relief Committee and East End Welfare Board." Of these two groups, the Red Cross probably wielded the most power, primarily owing to the funds which they had available. Unfortunately, little is known about the East End Welfare Board, but in all likelihood it was primarily an agency of organization and coordination of post-riot activities and strategy in black Tulsa. "These men worked faithfully and have fought many battles for their fellowman," Mary E. Jones Parrish wrote of this group. "They looked after the needs of the people both physically and legally to the best of their ability, with the assistance of the outside world."[17]

Red Cross activities began in Tulsa on June 1, but it was not until a couple of days later that they received official sanction from the civilian authorities. Initially, its operations were headquartered in the

Looking toward "Deep Greenwood."
Courtesy of Western History Collections, University of Oklahoma Library

Part of the black business district.
Courtesy of the Metropolitan Tulsa Chamber of Commerce

downtown area, but on June 3, an officer from the divisional headquarters in St. Louis arrived in Tulsa and moved the operational offices to the Booker T. Washington School. An emergency hospital, a
central first aid station, and a dispensary were also established at the
school, and the medical work performed there was a collaboration of
efforts between the Red Cross, local physicians, the County Superin-
tendent of Health, and the State of Oklahoma.[18]

By June 3, relief supplies were being given on a family basis, and
on June 7, the Red Cross announced that "it would assist only those
financially unable to bear the burden." Efforts were made by the organization and other groups to secure employment for black Tulsans
rendered jobless by the riot. The Red Cross made the homeless who
were employed pay for meals, but for some time fed the unemployed

The remains of the "Negro Wall Street": looking north on
Greenwood Avenue from Archer.

and the ill for free. This latter group, along with women with in-
fants, were given relief supplies, but the mode of distribution soon
changed from actual handouts to "clothing and grocery permits."
Black women and some black children were given cloth and provided with sewing machines with which to make clothing and bedding. The Red Cross was also instrumental in securing tents for
black Tulsans whose homes had been destroyed. Governor Robertson, who had refused the offer of fifty Black Cross nurses by the president of the Chicago chapter of the Universal Negro Improvement
Association, also refused to consign some one hundred National
Guard tents for use in Tulsa. Although, by the first week in July the
Red Cross was feeding only those blacks who were ill, their relief
work in Tulsa did not end until December of 1921. It should not be
assumed that all black Tulsans accepted aid from the Red Cross, nor
that the organization was not viewed without suspicion. Mary E.
Jones Parrish, who was later loud in praise for the "Mother of the
World," at first avoided Red Cross workers.[19]

Some money and other donations also came into Tulsa from out of
town. Civic organizations from various other Oklahoma towns and
cities sent clothing and other articles. The NAACP initiated a nationwide campaign to raise money for the victims of the riot. It collected at least $1,900 for its "Tulsa Relief and Defense Fund," and its
contributions ranged from one dollar from a New Jersey woman, to
nearly $350 from the Los Angeles Branch of the NAACP. In addition
to sending money, the Colored Women's Branch of the New York
City YMCA also sent two barrels of clothing, which the express
company shipped free of charge.[20]

As important as these actions by non-Tulsans were, there was a
much more powerful and ominous force working within Tulsa
which shaped its post-riot history: the city's official "relief" activities as carried out by the Executive Welfare Committee and its
successor, the Reconstruction Committee. The former was organized, at the request of Adjutant General Barrett, on June 2 at a special meeting of the board of directors of the Tulsa Chamber of Commerce. It was authorized to "appoint such sub-committees as might
be necessary in the rehabilitation work and in bringing Tulsa back to

normalcy."[21] Before this meeting adjourned, Alva J. Niles, president of the Chamber of Commerce, read a statement concerning the riot which he had given to the press. In it, Niles stated:

> Leading business men are in hourly conference and a movement is now being organized, not only for the succor, protection and alleviation of the sufferings of the negroes, but to formulate a plan of reparation in order that homes may be re-built and families as nearly as possible rehabilitated. The sympathy of the citizenship of Tulsa in a great way has gone out to the unfortunate law abiding negroes who have become the victims of the action, and bad advice of some of the lawless leaders, and as quickly as possible rehabilitation will take place and reparation made. . . .
> Tulsa feels intensely humiliated and standing in the shadow of this great tragedy pledges its every effort to wiping out the stain at the earliest possible moment and punishing those guilty of bringing the disgrace and disaster to this city.

Niles ended his statement by citing Tulsa's war effort accomplishments, such as the Liberty Loan drive, as evidence that the "city can be depended upon to make a proper restitution and to bring order out of chaos at the earliest possible moment."[22]

A similar attitude was expressed by L. J. Martin, chairman of the Executive Welfare Committee. Martin was quoted in the *Independent* as stating: "Tulsa can only redeem herself from the country-wide shame and humiliation in which she is today plunged by complete restitution of the destroyed black belt. The rest of the United States must know that the real citizenship of Tulsa weeps at this unspeakable crime and will make good the damage, so far as can be done, to the last penny."[23]

This was not, however, the course of action which the Executive Welfare Committee took, and in light of what this committee actually did do, few statements about the riot are as hideously ludicrous as these made by Niles and Martin. On June 4, there was a meeting between the Executive Welfare Committee—which, like the Chamber of Commerce, had no black members—and other white "relief" groups. They decided not to solicit any funds for aid, "but that any offers in the form of cash would be accepted by the Red Cross and used for relief work." Furthermore, and most importantly, "it was decided not to accept any other kind of donation nor would any help, financial or otherwise, be accepted to reconstruct the Negro district."[24]

Thus, while the officials of the Tulsa Chamber of Commerce were telling the nation's press that reparation and restitution would be made, they charted a directly opposite course, even to the point of refusing offers of aid for people whom they hardly represented. One Chamber of Commerce member stated that "numerous telegrams were received by the executive committee from various cities in the Union offering aid, but the policy was quickly adopted that this was strictly a Tulsa affair and that the work of restoration and charity would be taken care of by Tulsa people." This supports a statement made by Walter White that outsiders made offers of money to be used in relief work in Tulsa—including a $1,000 offer of aid from the Chicago *Tribune*—but that the parties were told "in theatric fashion that the citizens of Tulsa 'were to blame for the riot and that they themselves would bear the costs of restoration.'"[25]

On June 14, Mayor Evans appointed a Reconstruction Committee, approved by the City Commission, to carry out his plans for the "reconstruction" of black Tulsa, and to direct the city's official post-riot policies. The next day, the members of the Executive Welfare Committee tendered their resignations to the board of directors of the Chamber of Commerce, their authority in "relief" work having been negated by the action of the City Commission.[26] However, one week earlier, two actions occurred which provide yet another view of the "relief" intentions of the local white powers and elite.

The first was mentioned in the June 7 report of the Executive Welfare Committee, in which it informed the public that, under its direction, "the Real Estate Exchange was organized to list and appraise the value of properties in the burned area and to work out a plan of possible purchase and the conversion of the burned area into an industrial and wholesale district." This plan received the support of certain white civic organizations, businessmen, and political elements, and the Executive Welfare Committee took some steps toward establishing a group to buy the land from black owners.[27]

The other action of June 7, motivated by similar desires, was the passage of Fire Ordinance No. 2156 by the City Commission. Under its provisions, several blocks of the burned black district which had been partially, if not totally, destroyed were now made part of the "official" fire limits of the City of Tulsa. This was not an issue of small consequence to black Tulsans, nor was it by any means a gesture of kindness toward them, for any structure within the city's "official" fire limits had to be constructed of concrete, brick, or steel, and had to be at least two stories high. The effect of the ordinance was to prevent some black Tulsans from rebuilding their burned homes where they had been. Walter White observed that the ordinance was passed "for the purpose of securing possession of the land at a low figure," and that "white business men" had been trying to obtain this land for years.[28]

That Mayor Evans particularly favored these actions is best evident in his June 14 message to the City Commission. "Let the negro settlement be placed farther to the north and east," Evans stated, citing his belief that "a large portion of this district is well suited for industrial purposes than for residences." The mayor of Tulsa also urged the commissioners to take action quickly: "We should immediately get in touch with all the railroads with a view to establishing a Union station on this ground. The location is ideal and all the railroads convenient."[29] Whether or not the Executive Welfare Committee and Mayor Evans had been working in conjunction prior to this meeting of the City Commission, it is quite evident that they were basically expressing the same designs for black Tulsa.

Some of the directors of the Chamber of Commerce—some of whom had been members of the Executive Welfare Committee— eventually turned against these plans. On July 1, the Chamber's board of directors approved a resolution of the city's Reconstruction Committee that a union railway station project be explored, but omitted "the recommendation of any particular location for the terminal." Two weeks later, a black man appeared before the board and informed them that under the present rulings it was not possible for black Tulsans to build on their own property. He also stated that "as winter is rapidly approaching it is necessary that the construction of homes begin at once." After "considerable discussion," the board of directors appointed a five-man committee to investigate the issue. Four days later, this special committee submitted a report which stated:

> That the paramount issue at this time is the housing and rehabilitation of the negroes.
> That while the Union Station project and industrial district may be desirable at some further time, the agitation of the same now is not germain [*sic*] to the issue.
> That in order to enable the negro property owner to help himself he should be allowed to immediately house himself and family on his property.
> We, therefore, recommend that permission be granted by the city to the negroes to build on their own property as a solution of the problem facing the city at this time.

The report was eventually submitted to the Reconstruction Committee, who rejected its recommendations.[30]

Sympathy for the dilemma that black Tulsans faced was not, however, the only reason why some of the members of the Chamber's board of directors eventually turned "against" the plans of the Executive Welfare Committee, the city government, and other white groups to secure land in black Tulsa for the construction of a railroad terminal. In August, Colonel Reeves of the board stated:

> We must forget the causes of the riot and find a solution that will be basically right. We must determine whether this area is physically suited for a terminal point. Even if it is a terminal point, we are not ready to condemn it for a terminal point. We can not condemn property for factory sites. Railroad engineers will look to the physical site only. I suggest that cheap shacks be constructed rather than 6, 8 or 10 story buildings, because when the proper time comes to condemn it it will be possible to finance the proceedings. At the present time we must abandon the idea of buying this property for factory and warehouse sites because we have no corporation formed to buy this land.

He added one more reason: "If we had a company formed it would still be impossible to buy this land for a certain percentage of the negroes would not sell."[31]

Black Tulsans were far from silent on this issue, and it was only their action which prevented this further attempt by white Tulsans to destroy their community. A protest was presented to the City

B. C. Franklin, right, one of the attorneys who helped to defeat the city's fire ordinance.

Courtesy of Mrs. Mozella Jones

Commission on July 28 by property owners "against the closing of Haskell Street" opposite the Booker T. Washington School. On August 26 another petition, which was duly received and filed, was presented to the commissioners "of residents and property owners for repealing or modification of the Ordinance relating to the fire limits, and by so doing give permission to rebuild destroyed property in the Burned Area."[32] Evidence suggests that the East End Welfare Board was also involved in these actions against the new fire ordinance.[33]

The action which ultimately decided the dispute over the fire ordinance was the lawsuit filed in district court on August 1 by the black Tulsa law firm of P. A. Chappelle, I. H. Spears, and B. C. Franklin. The case, *Joe Lockett* v. *the City of Tulsa* requested permission for Lockett to rebuild and for the court to enjoin the city from enforcing its new ordinance. The black Tulsans won their suit some three weeks later, when three judges declared the ordinance void on the grounds that it took private property without due process of law.[34]

This defeated move for a new railroad station and the relocation of black Tulsa was the substance of the initiatory post-riot policies of Mayor Evans, the City Commission, and the Reconstruction Committee. This is hardly surprising, especially when one considers Evans' public statements about the riot. In his June 14 message to the City Commission, in which he clearly blamed black Tulsans for the riot, Evans implied that the destruction of most of black Tulsa during the riot may have been a good thing for the city! Much in the manner that some city officials had felt that the lynching of Roy Belton would prove "beneficial" to Tulsa, the Mayor stated:

> It is in the judgement of many wise heads in Tulsa, based upon a number of years, that this uprising was inevitable. If that be true and this judgement had to come upon us, then I say it was good generalship to let the destruction come to that section where the trouble was hatched up, put in motion and where it had its inception. . . .
>
> All regret the wrongs that fell upon the innocent negroes and they should receive such help as we can give them if within our power. It, however, is true of any warfare that the fortunes of war fall upon the innocent along with the guilty. This is true of any conflict, invasion or uprising. Think of what would have happened had the Allies marched to Berlin.

The mayor's message was endorsed by all of the city commissioners except C. S. Younkman.[35]

The Reconstruction Committee was officially in operation until January, 1922, but little was discovered of its activities after the fire ordinance was declared unconstitutional. The actions of the City Commission concerning the riot were primarily responsive in nature. It disallowed, and in a few rare cases, allowed, claims against the city for losses incurred during the riot. In July, 1921, it responded to a Red Cross report of unsanitary conditions in the burned district by investigating the matter, and then allowed up to $700 to be spent for toilet facilities. The Commission granted a request by a group of black plumbers that they temporarily be given plumber's permits without cost. In a few instances, primarily in the removal of trash and debris, the Commission may have initiated action—but even then such motions were in response to the actions and desires of others.[36] Thus, taken as whole, the primary post-riot policies of Tulsa's white authorities were to first give the impression to the rest of the nation that white Tulsa would make reparations and rebuild the burned black district, and then to unsuccessfully attempt to prevent black Tulsans from rebuilding their community where it had been.

IV

The dislocation of black Tulsa that the riot caused was immense. One-half of the city's black population was forcibly interned for varying lengths of time. When they gained their release, many of these people found that their homes had been destroyed. Most had to live with friends or relatives, or simply make do the best they could. Some left town for good, and of them, historian Henry Whitlow has stated: "According to the Tulsa *Tribune*—on the night of the riot and immediately thereafter, many Negroes moved from Tulsa and never returned. But as has been said, locally, those that left were afraid and/or tired of living under conditions that existed in Tulsa. However, those that stayed were unafraid and were determined to make living conditions better. They began to rebuild."[37]

The erection of tents and shacks in the burned areas of black Tulsa began when blacks were allowed to return, and probably increased considerably by mid-June, at which time most black Tulsans had been released by the white authorities. Over 350 tents were erected during the first week, some of which had wooden floors and screen doors. Although some of these tents were provided by local businessmen, the lion's share was initially supplied by the Red Cross.[38]

The fire ordinance passed by the City Commission slowed the rebuilding process. Upon request of the Red Cross, which was possibly working in conjunction with the East End Welfare Board, the Commission at first allowed blacks to construct temporary structures upon those lots within the new fire limits, but they rescinded their permission one week later. Some clandestine rebuilding took place while the fire ordinance was in force. When the ruling against the ordinance was handed down on September 1, the rate of rebuilding had assuredly increased, as the cold weather was fast approaching.

Although City Commission records reveal that a few people appeared before that body to seek permission to rebuild, it is possible that many others worked solely through Building Inspector H. E. Kopp and Fire Marshal Wesley Bush.[39]

Even though a fair amount of rebuilding had taken place by the beginning of autumn, conditions were extremely harsh for the mass of black Tulsans. The actions of the Chamber of Commerce and the City Commission had made preparations for the ensuing winter months nearly impossible. On October 25, Walter White wrote: "Practically all of the colored citizens who remain in Tulsa are living in tents and a few boarded shacks [which] have been constructed through the Red Cross and through contributions made by this Association [NAACP]. In a letter we have just received from Tulsa, it is stated that few of the citizens have any protection from the weather and that there will be many deaths from pneumonia, influenza and exposure during the coming winter because of the failure of the white citizens of Tulsa to keep their promises."[40]

Something approaching one thousand black Tulsans spent the winter of 1921–1922 in tents.[41] By the summer of 1922, all black Tulsans were said to be living in "wooden buildings," and during that year, brick buildings once again began to line Greenwood Avenue. Slowly, but surely, black Tulsa prospered again.[42]

A few days after the riot, the Tulsa *World* had written:

> Vandalism has taken the homes and savings of thousands of people. Tulsa must restore that which has been taken. The sins of a comparative few are thus visited upon a whole community. But it is a cross that must be shouldered willingly and heroically. This restitution, not because of affectionate regard for the colored man, but because of an honorable and intense regard for the white race whose boast of superiority must now be justified by concrete acts.
>
> Not else can the wounds of passion be healed or the scars of intolerant hatred be soothed. In this moment men of Tulsa stand at the crossroads in the city's destiny. There must not, there cannot, be any hesitating.[43]

This opinion that Tulsa, meaning *white* Tulsa, must rebuild the burned black district was echoed by the *Tribune*, and voiced, as we have seen, by "prominent" white Tulsans such as L. J. Martin and Alva J. Niles. This is not to suggest that the *World*, the *Tribune*, ex-

Mayor Martin, nor the Chamber of Commerce spoke for *all* of white Tulsa, for they clearly did not (they being more representative of the city's upper and middle class whites).[44]

The fact is that, contrary to these announced intentions in the *World* and elsewhere, white Tulsans did not rebuild black Tulsa. Indeed, as has been shown, the city government and other white groups tried to prevent it. Any role which local whites had in the rebuilding came through three indirect avenues. First, there were some local donations to the Red Cross. Second, some whites were property owners in black Tulsa, and these people rebuilt the destroyed structures on the land which they owned—in order to once again collect rent from black tenants. And lastly, some whites loaned money to black employees for rebuilding purposes.

An early tent, right, where homes had been.
Courtesy of the Metropolitan Tulsa Chamber of Commerce

This is an extremely complex question, but extensive research on it has led me to the conclusion that the white role in the rebuilding of black Tulsa has been grossly exaggerated. The $26,000 that the Executive Welfare Committee turned over to the Red Cross was collected (under the direction of C. S. Avery) probably, though not necessarily, in large part from white Tulsans, and it is conceivable that some of it may have been used for rebuilding purposes. Many whites were property owners in the burned district, and pending further research, one must conclude that they played a hand in the rebuilding of their property. There were a couple of other exceptions, including a house built for blacks in the burned district by the Gypsy Oil Company. Aside from the $11,400 which the City Commission paid the Red Cross for "expenditures made on account of the riot of May 31 and June 1, 1921," there is not much evidence for any substantial, direct role played by the city in the reconstruction of black Tulsa. It allocated some provisions for sanitation, such as trash removal, plumbing, and scavenger work (who was to reap the benefits of this is unclear), but this had little to do with the actual rebuilding of the destroyed area.[45] On the whole, it is evident that white Tulsans had only a minimal role in the rebuilding of the devastated area.

Mary E. Jones Parrish, writing about the East End Welfare Board, succinctly stated that "it was through the inspiration supplied by this committee, working in harmony with the Red Cross, that Greenwood has been rebuilt today." Yet, except in that the East End Welfare Board may have been the recipient of donations from the NAACP and others, this group probably lacked any real funds of its own, and its role in the rebuilding must be placed in perspective. Rather, the Board appears largely to have been an important agent in the organization of black responses to local white "relief" policies, and in the direction of legitimate relief efforts. The Red Cross, however, had a larger treasury to draw from and it expended some funds for the rebuilding of black Tulsa. When the organization terminated its relief work in the city at a program given on Christmas Eve, 1921, it had expended over $100,000. The Red Cross had employed an average of fifteen carpenters during the preceding three months "to help widows, the ill and the physically handicapped" to rebuild. In addition, the organization had purchased and furnished some building

While Tulsa's white leaders assured the rest of the nation that the city would rebuild the destroyed black district, locally they charted a directly opposite course. Something approaching one thousand black Tulsans were forced to spend the winter of 1921–1922 living in tents.

Courtesy of the Metropolitan Tulsa Chamber of Commerce

supplies—part of which had been donated by some lumber and hardware dealers—which included "some three-hundred and seventy-thousand square feet of lumber, over sixteen thousand feet of screen wire and thousands of dollars worth of other materials."[46]

Yet, as important as these donations were, the role of the Red Cross, too, must be viewed in perspective. Property losses in black Tulsa due to the riot ran into the millions of dollars. While many black Tulsans were aided in some form by the Red Cross, many others were not. The primary problem which all black Tulsans faced who had lost their homes and their businesses in the riot was where to secure the capital to rebuild. Tulsa historian Henry Whitlow has suggested that some "began to rebuild with private funds and many borrowed money out of town and out of state." It was ironically fortunate that "Deep Greenwood" did not include a bank in the spring of 1921, for it, too, would have surely been destroyed by the white rioters. Some black Tulsans had money in white banks downtown, which they used to rebuild. Who rebuilt black Tulsa? In the end, black Tulsans themselves, with some help from outside sources, must be credited with the reconstruction of their community—at interest. And in a spirit reminiscent of the American frontier, at times they combined their labor in the rebuilding of each other's homes.[47]

## V

When Governor James B. A. Robertson visited Tulsa on June 2, 1921, he ordered that a grand jury be impaneled to make a thorough investigation of the riot. District Judge W. Valjean Biddison was named the presiding jurist, and State Attorney General S. P. Freeling—assisted by Kathryn Van Leuven—was to officiate in the investigations. Robertson, who said that he was "determined that the cause of this riot shall be ascertained and that the responsibility for the same fixed and the guilty parties brought to justice," instructed Freeling to go to Tulsa at once to preserve and gather evidence for the grand jury. Furthermore, the governor told the attorney general, "If, in your opinion the facts warrant, the peace officers who are charged with the duty of maintaining order should be removed from office."[48]

The jurors for the grand jury were selected by June 9. Four days later, it published a call in the newspapers for all to come and testify who so desired. In its twelve-day session, the grand jury initiated some twenty-seven cases, which indicted over eighty-five persons.[49] On June 25, it handed down its final report. Although the report condemned the "exaggerated and untrue reports of the press, purporting to give the facts, both as to the cause and to the result of the riot," in it the grand jury—like virtually every other group of white Tulsans —clearly blamed black Tulsans for the riot:

> We find that the recent race riot was the direct result of an effort on the part of a certain group of colored men who appeared at the courthouse on the night of May 31, 1921, for the purpose of protecting one Dick Rowland then and now in the custody of the sheriff of Tulsa county for an alleged assault upon a young white woman. We have not been able to find any evidence either from white or colored citizens that any organized attempt was made or planned to take from the sheriff's custody any prisoner; the crowd assembed about the courthouse being purely spectators and curiosity seekers resulting from rumors circulated about the city. There was no mob spirit among the whites, no talk of lynching and no arms. The assembly was quiet until the arrival of the armed negroes, which precipitated and was the direct cause of the entire affair.

Although the grand jury reiterated its claim that the "presence of the armed negroes" was the direct cause of the riot, they further claimed that "there existed indirect causes more vital to the public interest than the direct cause." Among them, the report asserted, "were agitation among the negroes of social equality, and the laxity of law enforcement on the part of the officers of the city and county."[50]

The report claimed that "certain propaganda and more or less agitation had been going on among the colored population for some time," and that this had resulted "in the accumulation of firearms among the people and the storage of quantities of ammunition, all of which was accumulative in the minds of the negro which led them as a people to believe in equal rights, social equality and their ability to demand the same." The grand jury further stated, "We are glad to exonerate the great majority of the colored people who neither had knowledge of nor part in . . . the accumulation of arms and ammunition," but added that they had sought to "ascertain the names of the particular parties who took part and the indictments returned show our findings."[51]

Many of the recommendations which the grand jury presented to the public concerned what they felt to be the gross laxity of law enforcement in Tulsa County, with "laws being openly violated in many ways, by and with the consent, if not even the assistance, of the officers." In one recommendation along these lines, a plea was made for stricter law enforcement, while in another, the grand jury asked for further racial segregation:

> We find that police protection with negro policemen as officers has been insufficient; that violations of the law have been condoned and while raids have been made and also some arrests, the same offense by the same offender was repeated almost immediately. We therefore recommend that "colored town" be policed by white officers, that indiscriminate mingling of white and colored people in dance halls and other places of amusement be positively prohibited and every law rigidly enforced in the end that a proper relationship may be maintained between the two races, and that every safeguard that may be had for the positive protection of life and property everywhere.[52]

On the one hand, the report stated, "We believe, however, that law violations have not been contained to the colored district, but that the 'choc' joints and 'houses of prostitution' are more or less common in the city of Tulsa as well as in the county." Nevertheless, the grand jury was anxious that the exact *opposite* impression be given to outsiders.

> It is the observation of the public as well as members of the grand jury that the appearance of traffic policemen at street crossings dressed in "short sleeves" with a gun on his "hip" tends to give impression to the ouside world of a spirit of lawlessness which does not exist. It is the conviction of the grand jury that if the safety of the public demands a traffic policeman to carry a gun on his hip, courtesy to the public should also require that any policeman wearing a gun should in every case be required to wear a coat to the end that no false impression be given to the general public or to the outside world.

The report of the grand jury concluded with a plea to the public to take an active interest in "selecting and electing men and women of ability and character who desire to make Tulsa fit for the home of the most respectable, home loving and law abiding citizens in America."[53]

State Attorney General Freeling was not at all pleased with this report. According to *Harlow's Weekly*, an Oklahoma magazine, "he refused to have anything to do with this report and in open court after conducting the preceedings of the grand jury he expressed his dissatisfaction at the result of its investigation." Little action was taken by the state, however.[54]

The twenty-seven cases that the grand jury initiated too ended for the most part in inaction. The charges filed were for riot in seven of these cases, for grand larceny in twelve, and for arson in two. The other six each involved a different charge, including assault with attempt to kill, pointing a pistol at another person, and the case involving Dick Rowland and Sarah Page, with Rowland being charged with attempt to rape. Perhaps the most important of these cases was the first one initiated by the grand jury, that of the *State of Oklahoma* v. *Will Robinson, et al.* In this case, some fifty-seven persons, apparently all of them black, were charged with rioting. Those charged included A. J. Smitherman, editor of the Tulsa *Star*, and J. K. Smitherman, a deputy sheriff.[55]

Court records reveal that twenty of these cases were definitely dismissed, at least eighteen of them by the motion of the county attorney. A motion to dismiss the Robinson case was filed on November 22, 1922, and it too was apparently dismissed. Five of the remaining six seem never to have gotten off the ground because the bench warrants which were issued for them were never served. The final case was also probably dismissed, or simply allowed to die.[56]

Police Chief Gustafson was suspended from office by Judge Biddison and was later found guilty on two counts—"failure to take proper precautions for the protection of life and property during the riot and conspiracy to free automobile thieves and collect rewards." One black Tulsan may have been sentenced to thirty days in the county jail for allegedly carrying a concealed weapon, but *no* white Tulsans were ever sent to prison for the killing, burning, and looting of the race riot of 1921.[57]

There was one other detail. Sarah Page refused to prosecute and Dick Rowland was exonerated.[58]

Chapter 5
# The Segregation
# of Memory _____

It is part of our nature as human beings—whether as individuals, groups, or societies—that we create "pasts" with which we can live. If the reality of our history poses questions about our lives of today which are too painful or ominous to ponder, then we will mold our past into a less threatening chronicle, or repress it entirely. If anything, our "historic memory" is as malleable as our personal one. Thus the way in which the Tulsa race riot is remembered speaks to us as much about the Tulsa and America of today as it does about the events of 1921. The historical context of the riot and the scope of its effects must therefore be considered alongside the direct investigation of events and responses.

I

What is to be made of the madness that was the Tulsa riot of 1921? The forces which helped to create it were many. Some of them affected the entire nation; others affected only Oklahoma; some were peculiar to Tulsa.

The various racial ideologies which were being popularized nationally helped to breed situations in which large-scale racial violence could incubate. By the time of the riot, Tulsa had become a bastion of Ku Klux Klan strength in the Southwest. The mythical "reconstruction" of black Tulsa by politically and socially influential white Tulsans, be they members of the hooded order or not, revealed a total disregard for the rights of black citizens.[1]

Concomitantly, the actions of those black Tulsans who defended their homes, businesses, fellow citizens, and families were tangible examples of the doctrine of a steadfast self-defense which many black Americans were advocating. Such a doctrine had long been a part of black history, but the contradictions raised by the black experience in the First World War, coupled with the acute rise of white violence, increased its importance during the immediate postwar years. Indeed, O. W. Gurley, an affluent black Tulsan who suffered heavy losses due to the riot, laid much of the blame for the violence on the group of blacks who went down to the courthouse. The leader of this group, Gurley stated, was a tall man "who came back from France with exaggerated ideas of equality."[2] The Tulsa riot, along with the other race riots of the postwar period, was in one sense a physical realization of some of the major black and white racial ideologies of the era.

The political currents flowing through Oklahoma during this period were also important. The decline of a major political organization in the state, the Oklahoma Socialist party, which was at least rhetorically supportive of black rights, and the rapid rise of another, the Ku Klux Klan, which was clearly anti-black, was not without significance. But neither political development explains why the riot happened. Rather, they were indicative of a more basic ideological shift within the state and region. Dallas and Shreveport, for example, were other centers of Klan strength in the Southwest, yet neither of them experienced racial violence on the scale of Tulsa during this period. The nationwide recession of 1921, which severely affected Tulsa, may have also played a role in increasing social tension, but economic woes do not by themselves create racial violence, as the experience of the Great Depression of the 1930s revealed.[3]

Tulsa's vice conditions and the nature of its local law enforcement were highly relevant. Five weeks before the riot, in April, 1921, a federal agent visited Tulsa undercover to investigate crime conditions in the city. In his report, he stated:

> Summary of conditions: Vice conditions in this city are very bad. Gambling, bootlegging and prostitution are very much in evidence. At the leading hotels and rooming houses the bell hops and porters are pimping

for women, and also selling booze. Regarding violations of the law these prostitutes and pimps solicit without any fear of the police, as they will invariably remind you that you are safe in these houses.[4]

The abundance of crime in Tulsa, coupled with the extremely selective nature of the city's law enforcement, helped to create a situation where the role of the police in the actual policing of the city was ill-defined.[5]

This situation was further exacerbated by the city's "vigilante" tradition. The incident involving the seventeen IWW members revealed much more to the community than the rabid hysteria of the wartime Tulsa *World* or Judge Evans' total disregard for legal justice. It also showed the city that even when a guilty verdict was brought in against accused persons, the Tulsa police force could not be depended upon to protect them. This fact, joined with the rising number of lynchings of blacks in Oklahoma, pointed to the involvement of the city police force in a more generalized civic ethos of anti-black, anti-radical militance. If the incident involving the alleged assailants of O. W. Leonard in 1919 temporarily calmed black fears, the lynching of Roy Belton in 1920 merely reconfirmed them: no accused blacks were safe in the hands of the white law enforcement officials in Tulsa. The black distrust of white police only increased when white officers began to invade black Tulsa and harass its citizens. Only the mode of white aggression was new. The style had long been a part of the local custom.[6]

The incident between Dick Rowland and Sarah Page, whatever the actual circumstances may have been, was important, but the affair needs to be placed in perspective. It seems highly probable that almost any other alleged "serious crime" involving a black "assailant" and a white "victim" could have played the catalytic role that the Rowland-Page incident did. The Leonard affair revealed that some black Tulsans were very concerned over the relatively "mild" newspaper coverage of such an alleged crime. The incident also made it clear that black Tulsans were prepared to act forthrightly to ensure that accused members of their race were guaranteed a courtroom trial. And if Roy Belton had been black, he probably would have been lynched sooner. But the incident in the Drexel building had an important interracial sexual dynamic, and the white taboo regarding black men and white women was probably particularly strong in this area where there were a significant number more males than females. During this period the state was shifting from a primarily immigrant population to a temporarily more stable one, but still in the older age groups the disproportion between the sexes was as high as three to two.[7]

With all these related but subsidiary dynamics placed into perspective, it is clear that the single most important precipitating ingredient in the Tulsa race riot was the manner in which the Tulsa *Tribune* "covered" the Rowland-Page incident. Indeed, the newspaper's specific coverage, and not what actually transpired in the Drexel building, is *the* incident. Whether or not a complete copy of the May 31, 1921, issue of the *Tribune* may surface again, there is a fair amount of evidence as to what it did contain, and its role in the creation of the race riot was noted by both blacks and whites, including the white adjutant general of Oklahoma.[8] The *Tribune*, through its May 31 issue, was the single most important force in the creation of the lynch mob outside of the courthouse; anything Dick Rowland might have done was secondary. In many ways the role of the *Tribune* is directly comparable to that of the *World* in the 1917 incident involving that attack on the seventeen IWW members.

Yet, though the *Tribune* clearly helped mobilize the lynch mob and thus directly contributed to the race riot, the Tulsa Police Department and the Tulsa County Sheriff's Office were also important factors. The law enforcement authorities knew the purpose of the white crowd outside of the courthouse. If these authorities had taken steps to prevent the crowd from forming, or if they had dispersed it once it had formed, the riot might have been averted. Here, Chief Gustafson was particularly at fault as it appears that Sheriff McCullough was attempting to make an honest effort to defend Rowland with his small force of men. Similarly, the predominantly white police force must also share heavily in the blame for the destruction of black Tulsa. Had their efforts, and those of the other law enforcement bodies, including the National Guard, been geared toward disarming and dispersing the white rioters, rather than disarming and interning blacks, much of the black district might have been saved. The mass deputizing of whites from the lynch mob by the police only encouraged the devastation.

The attempted intervention of those armed black Tulsans who went down to the courthouse was another ingredient in the riot, but to claim that they "caused" the race riot, as many have, is absurd. It is part of the nature of racism that hatred directed against an individual can very easily be translated into hatred against that person's entire race. The *Tribune's* coverage of the Rowland-Page incident had helped to facilitate this shift with its headline: "Nab *Negro* for Attacking *Girl* in Elevator."[9] But it was at the courthouse where the "immediate" hatred of the whites shifted from being aimed solely at Dick Rowland to all blacks in general, and the actions of those blacks who attempted to intervene were instrumental in initiating this transformation. This shift was further aggravated by the courthouse battle which slowly wound its way to black Tulsa. When it reached the black neighborhoods, the conflict was no longer a white lynch mob against Rowland—and a black attempt to prevent it—but simply a case of white against black.

The social, political, and racial conditions in Tulsa in the spring of 1921 were clearly those which would allow large-scale racial violence, and the action or inaction of certain parts of the community on May 31 and June 1 "complemented" the underlying conditions and brought on the violence and destruction.

## II

Aside from the deaths, the human suffering, and the destruction, the riot had other effects. For one thing, it appears that there was never another attempt at lynching a black person in Tulsa County. Beatings and floggings, however, continued. In May of 1922 black Deputy Sheriff John K. Smitherman had one of his ears cut off by a group of masked whites. Less than a year and a half later, in August, 1923, a white Tulsan—a Jew—by the name of Nathan Hantaman was picked up and questioned by the Tulsa police under suspicion of being a narcotics seller, or so the police claimed. In a situation which bears much in common with the IWW case in 1917, Hantaman was later released, and, according to one historian, "by apparent prearrangement, snatched up from the street by the Klan" in front of a theater on Greenwood Avenue. He was then taken outside of town, "stripped, whipped, and his genitals beaten to a pulp." The incident itself became the catalyst for Oklahoma Governor John C. Walton's "war" on the Ku Klux Klan which did much to wreck the order both statewide and in Tulsa.[10] Nevertheless, the lynchings ceased; at a terrible price, black Tulsans had shown their white brethren that they were not going to let it happen here.

For some, the riot was a bearer of lessons. In her *Events of the Tulsa Disaster*, Mary E. Jones Parrish wrote what she felt they were:

> The Tulsa disaster has taught great lessons to all of us, has dissipated some of our false creeds, and has revealed to us verities of which we were oblivious. The most significant lesson it has taught me is that the love of race is the deepest feeling rooted in our being and no race can rise higher than its lowest member.
>
> Some of our group who have been blest with educational or financial advantages are oftimes inclined to forget ourselves to the extent that they feel their superiority over those less fortunate, but when a supreme test, like the Tulsa disaster comes, it serves to remind us that we are all of one race; that human fiends, like those who had full sway on June 1st, have no respect of person. Every Negro was accorded the same treatment, regardless of his education or other advantages. A Negro was a Negro on that day and forced to march with his hands up for blocks. What does this teach? It should teach us to "Look Up, Lift Up and Lend a Helping Hand," and remember that we cannot rise higher than our weakest brother.
>
> "Comfort the feeble minded; support the weak."
>
> I Thes. 5:14.[11]

Although in essence Parrish is calling here for black nationalism, the intimidation that her muted tone reveals alludes to an even greater problem faced by black Tulsans after the riot: how to survive. The actions of the city government, police, and elite business and commercial groups during the summer and winter of 1921 confirmed that this struggle would, if anything, be as hard as before.

Thus, as American blacks have done throughout their history, black Tulsans turned to themselves. For the first decade after the riot, it appears that the local churches, community groups, and simply the local networks of friendship and work place association of black Tulsans were the primary organizational means for coping with the issues of survival. It is true that a branch of the NAACP was formed in black Tulsa one year after the riot, but by 1926 a national officer for the organization wrote that the Tulsa Branch had been "dormant so long, I think it useless to make further inquiries regarding it." A new branch was not organized until 1930.[12]

### III

Perhaps the most lasting effects of the riot are the twin oral traditions—one set white and the other black—which it has generated in Tulsa decades later. The collective white "memory" of the riot in Tulsa has revealed both realism and fantasy, but in all cases, it has been subdued in one way or another. Those whites who were involved in the riot have been reluctant to discuss it—especially in the presence of a tape recorder—or have minimized their role. Fifty-seven years after the event, several white Tulsans allowed copies of old photographs of early Tulsa to be made, but adamantly refused to permit riot photographs to also be copied. White Tulsans too young to remember the event, or who were born after it, have often been able to spin tall tales about it.

A central feature of the local white oral tradition of the riot involves the cultivated ability which most white Americans have to blame other people for the racism and racial injustice which surrounds them. Primarily, blacks and other nonwhites are blamed, and as we have seen, black Tulsans have been blamed for the riot. But when white Americans are not faulting nonwhites for racial injustice, they blame *other* whites. Northern and western whites easily overlook the poverty—as well as the positive aspects—in their Harlems, Roxburys, and East Palo Altos and claim that only southern whites are racist. Southern ruling elites blame the "rednecks." And so forth. This ability to fault others has played a role in the mythology of the riot in white Tulsa, where today, among the upper and middle classes, it is said that the white rioters in 1921 were all "poor white trash." One local history buff even informed the author that the "white" rioters were Mexicans!

Although the specific historical evidence on who the white rioters were is far from great, that which we have is persuasive that no one "class" of whites had a monopoly. Photographs exist showing rioting whites dressed in the clothing of both businessmen and laborers.

The official dead and wounded tabulation of the police department for whites included a salesman, a barber, a tool dresser, and the manager of an oil company. Rather, it is likely that the white rioters came from all economic and social classes. Similarly, their victims ran the economic spectrum of black Tulsa, for as Mary E. Jones Parrish stated, "a Negro was a Negro on that day."[13]

The local white oral tradition of the riot also includes the events of its immediate aftermath. Indeed, many white Tulsans feel that the humanitarian actions of their forebears after the riot atoned for the involvement of whites in the violence itself. This has even worked its way into the popular historical literature about the riot: in 1976, one white woman wrote that within two days after the violence "white Tulsans had immediately begun a generous relief program."[14] The historical evidence, however, points to a vastly different conclusion. If anything, the aftermath of the riot was marked by a concerted attempt by white Tulsa's social and economic elite to further destroy the city's black community.

It should be pointed out that white Tulsans are hardly alone in this endeavor to "remember" their history, in Ralph Ellison's words, as that which they "would have liked to have been."[15] Rather, it is a characteristic of the oral historical tradition of most white Americans. That an institution as brutal as black slavery has been romanticized so often over the years is in itself a statement about the psychological needs of most white Americans in confronting—or rather, not confronting—their past.

Any similarities between the black and white oral traditions of the riot in Tulsa are far outweighed by their differences. Among black Tulsans, as well as among white Tulsans, the folklore of the event decades later includes both sober renditions and fantastical accounts of what transpired, and at least one folktale about the riot—one of which concerns "Peg Leg" Taylor, who is remembered by some for his work with black youth in Tulsa—has been collected and published. But unlike their white brethren, most black Tulsans who were involved in the riot have *not* been reluctant to discuss their experiences. This is because for many black Tulsans, the riot, and particularly the rebuilding of their community, is an issue of pride. Fifty years after the terrible spring of 1921, W. D. Williams—the young

Bill Williams in the Prelude—had a message for young black Tulsans: "They must remember that it was pride that started the riot, it was pride that fought the riot, it was pride that rebuilt after the riot, and if the same pride can again be captured among the younger Blacks, when new ideals with a good educational background, with a mind for business, 'Little Africa' can rise again as the Black Mecca of the southwest. But it is up to the young people." For others the memory of the riot has proved to be hardly an ennobling challenge. A black police officer related that his uncle, who had lived through the riot, still in 1978 kept a gun and ammunition in case it should happen again.[16]

It has been said in the city, by both blacks and whites, that the story of the riot has been "hushed up," and in fact during the 1950s and 1960s black civil rights leaders used the threat of "bringing up" the riot as leverage in negotiations with white leaders in Tulsa. Indeed, the most important factor seems to be what part of Tulsa one lives in. The Oklahoma *Eagle*, which has for many years been Tulsa's black newspaper, appears to have had no aversion to mentioning the riot over the decades, and in 1971 over two hundred black Tulsans commemorated the event with a ceremony. No such ceremony took place in white Tulsa that year, during which the Tulsa *Tribune* carried what was probably the first in-depth article on the riot since the 1920s. "For fifty years the *Tribune* did not rehash the story," this article concluded, "but the week of the 50th anniversary seems a natural time to relate just what did happen when a city got out of hand." The article made no mention of the role which the 1921 *Tribune* played in causing the riot.[17]

If the story has been suppressed, one reason would have to do with the very history of the city itself. Socially and politically prominent white Tulsans have always been especially sensitive about the city's image, a heritage dating from the early twentieth century when trainloads of "Tulsa Boosters" fanned out across the nation, trying to win new immigrants and convince people that Oklahoma was not a no man's land, but that young, beautiful Tulsa was a city bound for glory. If the national image of the city was brightened by these efforts, it was set back in the 1930s with the state's dust storms and migrants streaming west. Today, as Tulsa's claim to being the "Oil

Capital of the World" grows pretentious, some neo-boosters still bill Tulsa as "America's Most Beautiful City," an appellation given by *Reader's Digest* in the 1950s.[18] The race riot is, for some, a blot on the city's history and something not to be discussed, much less proclaimed.

A condition peculiar to but one American city? Hardly. Like the well-distributed history of racial violence in the United States, a segregation of memory exists in every part of the nation. It shall continue to do so as long as the injustice which has bred it continues.

IV

Beyond Tulsa, the immediate significance of the riot was perhaps greatest to the young state of Oklahoma. Of his youth in Oklahoma City, within one hundred miles of Tulsa, Ralph Ellison has written:

> We had a Negro church and a segregated school, a few lodges and fraternal organizations, and beyond those was the great white world. We were pushed off to what seemed the least desirable side of the city (but which years later was found to contain one of the state's richest pools of oil), and our system of justice was based upon Texas law, yet there was an optimism within the Negro community and a sense of possibility which, despite our awareness of limitation (dramatized so brutally in the Tulsa race riot of 1921), transcended all of this.[19]

In the aftermath of the Tulsa race riot, black Oklahomans employed their own resources, and in doing so, they have endured.

Yet, the event was not denied. If the early history of Oklahoma reveals a greater measure of black freedom and opportunity than the rest of the nation, then the Tulsa race riot—along with the Grandfather Clause, the increased lynchings of blacks, and the rise of Jim Crow—was a capstone to a movement to suppress any uniqueness in race relations which the young state had.

By the spring of 1921, Oklahoma had truly entered the Union.

Epilogue
# Notes on the Subsequent History of "Deep Greenwood"

The rebuilding of black Tulsa after the riot, particularly that of "Deep Greenwood," is a story of almost as great importance as the riot itself. Perhaps more than anything else, this rebuilding was a testament to the courage and stamina of Tulsa's black pioneers in their struggle for freedom.

Many of the buildings along the first block of Greenwood Avenue running north from Archer Street were rebuilt by the end of 1922. Although the burned-out shells of the pre-riot structures were for the most part torn down, many of the new buildings assumed the form of their predecessors. The 1922 Williams building, for example, bears a great resemblance to its pre-1921 predecessor. Many of these later buildings were constructed, as the original ones had been, with red bricks from a local brickyard located two blocks north on the avenue.[1]

"A little over a decade" after the riot, Henry Whitlow has written, "everything was more prosperous than before. Most of these businesses even survived the Depression." Furthermore, Whitlow tells us that a local Negro Business Directory was published, a Greenwood Chamber of Commerce organized, the National Negro Business League hosted here, and a black entrepreneur by the name of Simon Berry established a black-owned bus system. "Tulsa's Negro owned and operated business district became known nationally."[2]

Phoenix-like "Deep Greenwood" did not, however, prosper for-

A city reborn: looking north down Greenwood from Archer, 1938.
Courtesy of W. D. Williams

ever. By the end of World War II the district had begun a downward spiral. Again we turn to Whitlow: "The merchants of south Tulsa found that the dollar from Greenwood was just as green as the south of the tracks dollar. Relations became better . . . by the late fifties Greenwood was on the decline."[3]

"Greenwood won't be here any longer," Clarence Cherry told a journalist in 1971. "In a few years there won't be any Greenwood." Seven years later, Cherry's Shine Parlor is gone. So is the cafe, the nightclub, Jackson's barber shop, and the rooming house which lined the first block of Greenwood Avenue when Cherry reminisced.[4] In 1978, only two businesses, one of them the Oklahoma *Eagle*, remained. To be certain, the red brick buildings—many of them with cement datestones reading 1922—remain, but they are but empty ghosts of an earlier era.

Sitting in his sister's home in Tulsa, Dr. John Hope Franklin told the author, "There are two ways which whites destroy a black community. One is by building a freeway through it, the other is by changing the zoning laws." Along with the destruction of the 1921 riot, the first block of "Deep Greenwood" has, at least physically, survived this, too. Franklin's father helped to defeat the fire ordinance passed by the City Commission after the riot. In recent years, a freeway has cut through the section, but the first block of Green-wood Avenue remains. Few places in the city of Tulsa are as worthy

Greenwood and Archer, 1978.

of preservation as this first block of "Deep Greenwood," a monument to human endurance.

## Appendix I

Black Churches and Size of Congregation in Tulsa as Listed
by Tulsa City Directories, 1910–1914 and 1916–1922.

| Denomination | Congregation | Founded | '10 | '11 | '12 | '13 | '14 | '16 | '17 | '18 | '19 | '20 | '21 | '22 |
|---|---|---|---|---|---|---|---|---|---|---|---|---|---|---|
| Adventist | (Bethel) Seventh Day | 1918 | | | | | | | | | 26 | | 20 | 20 |
| Baptist | Bethelder | 1917 | | | | | | | | | 17 | 25 | 100 | 95 |
| | Macedonia/First | 1897 | * | * | * | * | 300 | 300 | 650 | 650 | 700 | 800 | 100 | 175[1] |
| | Metropolitan | 1917 | | | | | | | | | 154 | 168 | | 50 |
| | Morning Star | 1917 | | | | | | | | | 55 | 75 | * | * |
| | Mt. Zion | 1906 | * | | | * | 296 | 487 | 600 | 600 | 900 | 900 | 950 | 1,100 |
| | Paradise | 1913 | | | | | 35 | 35 | 50 | 50 | 50 | 70 | 83 | 83 |
| | Union Missionary | 1915 | | | | | | | 80 | | * | 40 | | |
| Christian | Christian Church | — | | | * | | | | | | | | | |
| Church of God | (308 N. Greenwood) | — | | | * | | | | | | | | | |
| | (1001 N. Greenwood) | 1916 | | | | | | | | | 55 | 70 | 70 | 70 |
| Church of God in Christ | (Independence St.) | 1910 | | | | | | | | | | | 140 | 125 |
| | (Greenwood Ave.) | 1917 | | | | | | | | | * | * | | 250 |
| Holiness | Apostolic | — | | | | | | | | | | | | |

113

| Methodist | | | | | | | | | | | | |
|---|---|---|---|---|---|---|---|---|---|---|---|---|
| | American | 1915 | | | | | | | | 100 | 125 | 150 |
| | Colored M. E. (Brown's Chapel) | 1908 | * | 50 | 60 | 104 | 173 | 173 | 295 | 300 | 350 | 275 |
| | Colored M. E. (Wesley's Chapel) | 1910 | * | 50 | 75 | 96 | 100 | 100 | 110 | 120 | 150 | 150 |
| | African M. E. (St. John's) | 1911 | * | | | | | | | | | * |
| | African M. E. (Vernon) | 1895 | * | 203 | 203 | 375 | 500 | 600 | 600 | 700 | 700 | 700 |
| Nazarene | Mission | 1920 | | | | | | | | | 12 | 150 |

* Asterisk denotes that the congregation was listed in that year's directory, but that the size of the congregation was not.

There were also a number of congregations which were listed in post-1922 city directories as having been founded prior to 1923, but do not appear in the directories for 1910–1914 and 1916–1922. These congregations are as follows (given with their supposed date of foundation):

Baptist: Mount Olive (1917); and Union (1916).
Christian: Madison Avenue (1917).
Church of God: Oklahoma Place (1911).
Church of God in Christ: Norfolk Avenue (1922).
Present Truth Mission (1922).

N.B.—In light of the fact that so many of the congregation size estimates are given in round numbers, it is highly possible that many of them are inflated.

[1] The figures for the size of the congregation of the Macedonia/First Baptist church for 1921 and 1922 may well be incorrect. Although they might truly represent a decline in membership due to the riot, the figures for the size of that congregation for 1923 and 1924—950 and 1,000, respectively—are more in line with the pre-1921 development, and cast some doubt on the 1921 and 1922 estimates.

# Appendix II

Black Business Establishments and Business Persons in Tulsa as Listed in Tulsa City Directories, 1907, 1909–1914, and 1916–1923.

| Establishments | '07 | '09 | '10 | '11 | '12 | '13 | '14 | '16 | '17 | '18 | '19 | '20 | '21 | '22 | '23 |
|---|---|---|---|---|---|---|---|---|---|---|---|---|---|---|---|
| Bath Parlors | | | | | | | | 1 | | | | | | | |
| Billiard Halls | | | 2 | 1 | 3 | 3 | 3 | 6 | 5 | 4 | 5 | 6 | 9 | 4 | 6 |
| Cigars and Tobacco | | | | | | | 1 | 2 | | | | 2 | | | |
| Clothing, Dry Goods, Racket, Second-hand, Music, Furniture, Paints and Oils, Shoes | | | 1 | 1 | 3 | 1 | 1 | | 2 | 2 | 2 | 1 | 2 | 2 | 2 |
| Confectionary, Soft Drinks | | | | 2 | 1 | 1 | 3 | 4 | 5 | 7 | 16 | 2 | 4 | 6 | 6 |
| Feed and Grain | | | | | | | | | | | 1 | 1 | 1 | 1 | 1 |
| Furnished Rooms, Boarding and Rooming Houses | 3 | | 2 | 3 | 2 | 1 | 4 | 3 | 1 | 6 | 5 | 9 | 11 | | 3 |
| Garages, Auto Repair and Filling Stations | 3 | 3 | 2 | | 1 | | 1 | 1 | 1 | | | 1 | 2 | | 3 |
| Grocers, Meat Markets | | | 2 | 5 | 8 | 10 | 9 | 7 | 18 | 11 | 21 | 23 | 41 | 34 | 31 |
| Hotels | | | | 1 | 2 | 1 | 1 | 1 | 1 | 2 | 2 | 4 | 5 | 4 | 9 |
| Restaurants | 1 | 1 | | 5 | 3 | 13 | 17 | 15 | 11 | 17 | 21 | 20 | 30 | 29 | 19 |
| Theaters | | | | | | 1 | | 1 | 1 | 1 | 1 | 1 | 2 | 1 | |
| Undertakers' Parlors | | | | | | | | 1 | 2 | 2 | 2 | 2 | 1 | 2 | 1 |
| *Total:* | 7 | 4 | 9 | 18 | 23 | 31 | 40 | 42 | 47 | 52 | 76 | 72 | 108 | 83 | 81 |

115

| Professionals | '07 | '09 | '10 | '11 | '12 | '13 | '14 | '16 | '17 | '18 | '19 | '20 | '21 | '22 | '23 |
|---|---|---|---|---|---|---|---|---|---|---|---|---|---|---|---|
| Dentists | | | | 1 | 1 | 1 | 1 | 1 | 1 | 1 | 1 | 3 | 2 | 2 | 2 |
| Druggists and Medicine Manufacturers | | 1 | | | 1 | 2 | | 1 | 4 | 3 | 3 | | 4 | 3 | 3 |
| Jewelers | | | | | | | | | | 1 | 1 | 1 | 1 | | |
| Lawyers | 1 | 1 | 3 | 4 | 2 | 1 | 5 | 6 | 4 | 4 | 5 | 4 | 3 | 4 | 6 |
| Nurses | | | | | | | | | | | | 2 | | 1 | |
| Photographers | | | | | | | | | | 1 | 1 | 1 | 2 | 1 | 2 |
| Physicians and Surgeons | 2 | 2 | 2 | 3 | 4 | 7 | 5 | 3 | 4 | 10 | 12 | 13 | 15 | 10 | 10 |
| Real Estate, Loans, and Insurance Agents | 2 | | | | | | 1 | 2 | 4 | 4 | 3 | 6 | 6 | 4 | 5 |
| Private Detectives | | | | | | | | | | | | | | | 1 |
| *Total:* | 5 | 4 | 5 | 8 | 8 | 11 | 13 | 13 | 17 | 23 | 26 | 30 | 33 | 25 | 30 |

| Skilled Crafts Persons | '07 | '09 | '10 | '11 | '12 | '13 | '14 | '16 | '17 | '18 | '19 | '20 | '21 | '22 | '23 |
|---|---|---|---|---|---|---|---|---|---|---|---|---|---|---|---|
| Bakers | | | | | | | | | | | | 1 | | | |
| Blacksmiths | | 1 | | | | 1 | 1 | 1 | 1 | 1 | 1 | | | 3 | 2 |
| Contractors, Carpenters, Builders, House and Sign Painters | | | | | | | | 1 | | 2 | 7 | 3 | 5 | 6 | 2 |
| Dressmakers | | | | | 1 | | | 1 | 1 | 3 | 4 | | 2 | 1 | 1 |
| Milliners | | | | | | | | | | | | | | | 1 |

| | '07 | '09 | '10 | '11 | '12 | '13 | '14 | '16 | '17 | '18 | '19 | '20 | '21 | '22 | '23 |
|---|---|---|---|---|---|---|---|---|---|---|---|---|---|---|---|
| Plumbers | | | | | | | | | | | 2 | | 1[1] | | |
| Printers | | | | | | | 1 | | 1 | 1 | 1 | | 1 | 1 | 1 |
| Shoemakers and Shoe Repairers | | | 2 | 2 | 1 | | 2 | 1 | 1 | | 3 | 2 | 4 | 6 | 3 |
| Tailors | | | | 1 | | 3 | 1 | 3 | 2 | 5 | 6 | 7 | 10 | 6 | 9 |
| Upholsterers | | | | | | | | | | 1 | | | 1 | 1 | |
| *Total:* | 1 | 2 | 3 | 1 | 3 | 6 | 7 | 5 | 15 | 22 | 14 | 24 | 24 | 24 | 19 |

[1] There is evidence in the Record of Commission Proceedings, City of Tulsa, Vol. XV, that there were a number more black plumbers in Tulsa in 1921.

| *Service Workers* | '07 | '09 | '10 | '11 | '12 | '13 | '14 | '16 | '17 | '18 | '19 | '20 | '21 | '22 | '23 |
|---|---|---|---|---|---|---|---|---|---|---|---|---|---|---|---|
| Barbers | 1 | 2 | 2 | 4 | 3 | 3 | 5 | 7 | 6 | 10 | 11 | 9 | 12 | 11 | 13 |
| Cleaners, Hatters, Dyers, and Pressers | | | 2 | 2 | 1 | 6 | 4 | 4 | 7 | 10 | 7 | 5 | 5 | 5 | 6 |
| Hairdressers | | | | | | | | 1 | | 3 | 3 | | 3 | | 1 |
| Launderers | | | | | | | 1 | | 1 | | | 1 | | 2 | 1 |
| Shoe Shiners | | | | | | | 2 | 2 | 5 | 4 | 6 | 4 | 6 | 6 | 1 |
| *Total:* | 1 | 2 | 4 | 6 | 4 | 9 | 12 | 14 | 19 | 27 | 27 | 19 | 26 | 24 | 22 |

| *Semi-Skilled Workers* | '07 | '09 | '10 | '11 | '12 | '13 | '14 | '16 | '17 | '18 | '19 | '20 | '21 | '22 | '23 |
|---|---|---|---|---|---|---|---|---|---|---|---|---|---|---|---|
| Expressmen and Messengers | | | | | | | 2 | 1 | | | | | | | |
| Housemovers | | | | | 1 | | | | | | | | | | |
| Newsdealers | | | | | 1 | | | | | | 1 | 1 | | 1 | 1 |
| *Total:* | | | | | 2 | | 2 | 1 | | | 1 | 1 | | 1 | 1 |

117

# NOTES _____

## PRELUDE In the Promised Land

1. For a discussion of the contents of the May 31, 1921, issue of the Tulsa *Tribune*, see pages 47–48, herein.
2. The primary source for this Prelude is an interview with W. D. Williams—"Bill" Williams—on June 7, 1978, in Tulsa.
3. A tabulation of racial violence in America which includes race riots is to be found in Richard Maxwell Brown, *Strain of Violence: Historical Studies of American Violence and Vigilantism* (New York: Oxford University Press, 1975), 320–26.
4. William Tuttle, *Race Riot: Chicago in the Red Summer of 1919* (New York: Atheneum, 1972), 268.

## Chapter 1: Boom Cities

1. United States Bureau of the Census, *Historical Statistics of the United States, Colonial Times to 1970, Bicentennial Edition, Part 1* (Washington D. C.: Government Printing Office, 1975), 24–37; Simon Kuznets and Dorothy Swaine Thomas, *Population Redistribution and Economic Growth: United States, 1870–1950, Vol. I* (Philadelphia: American Philosophical Society, 1957), 92.
2. William Butler, *Tulsa 75: A History of Tulsa* (Tulsa: Metropolitan Tulsa Chamber of Commerce, 1974), 27, 155; James Monroe Hall, *The Beginning of Tulsa* (Tulsa: Scott-Rice Company, 1928), 3; *1929 Consolidated Building Directory with City Map of Tulsa, Oklahoma* (n.p., n.p., n.d.), 1; *Tulsa City Directory, 1921* (Tulsa: Polk-Hoffhine Directory Company, 1921), 8.
3. A. V. Bourque, "The Story of Tulsa Is the Story of Oil," *Tulsa Spirit*, October, 1924, p. 16; C. Vann Woodward, *Origins of the New South, 1877–1913* (Baton Rouge: Louisiana State University Press, 1951), 302–303; Butler, *Tulsa 75*, 41.
4. Hall, *Beginning of Tulsa*, 3; Butler, *Tulsa 75*, 41, 45, 47.
5. Butler, *Tulsa 75*, 47, 49; Bourque, "The Story of Tulsa Is the Story of Oil," 16; Angie Debo, *Tulsa: From Creek Town to Oil Capital* (Norman: University of Oklahoma Press, 1943), 98.
6. In 1909, the city government purchased the bridge which spanned the Arkansas

River and established it as a "toll free route," thus further facilitating travel be-tween Tulsa and the nearby oil fields. Butler, *Tulsa 75*, 49, 156.

7. *Tulsa and West Tulsa, Oklahoma, Directory for 1909* (Tulsa: Burkhart Printing and Stationary Company, 1909), 16–22; Butler, *Tulsa 75*, 51–53.

8. Kuznets and Thomas, *Population Redistribution and Economic Growth*, I, 617, and III, 200.

9. Tulsa *World*, September 5, 1920, p. A2.

10. Debo, *Tulsa*, 44, 56–57. See also Arthur L. Tolson, *The Black Oklahomans: A History, 1541–1972* (New Orleans: Edwards Printing Company, 1972).

11. *Tulsa City Directory, 1916* (Tulsa: Polk-Hoffhine Directory Company, 1916), 34; *Tulsa City Directory, 1922* (Tulsa: Polk-Hoffhine Directory Company, 1922), 15. See Appendix I.

12. *Twelfth Census of the United States, 1900*, manuscript schedules for Tulsa, Creek County, Indian Territory, Vol. XV, 78A-89A, National Archives, Wash-ington, D.C.

13. Oklahoma *Eagle*, September 9, 1968, p. 14; Tulsa *World*, February 13, 1972, p. A8; Tulsa *Guide*, September 8, 1906, pp. 1–2; *Tulsa City Directory, 1907* (Tulsa: Tulsa OK Press, 1907), 17–24.

14. *Tulsa City Directories* for 1910, 1911, and 1913 (Tulsa: Polk-Hoffhine Directory Company, 1910–1913). Tulsa County's illiteracy rate for all blacks ten years old and older in 1910 was 8.3 percent, whereas the state and national rates for the same group were 17.7 percent and 30.4 percent, respectively. United States Bureau of the Census, *Negro Population, 1790–1915* (Washington, D.C.: Government Printing Office, 1918), 102, 404, 826–27; Tulsa *Weekly Planet*, July 18, 1912, p. 3. See Appendix II.

15. Henry Whitlow, "The History of the Greenwood Era in Tulsa," a paper presented to the Tulsa County Historical Society, March 29, 1973, p. 5. Greenwood Avenue most likely was named after Greenwood, Mississippi. Interview with W. D. Wil-liams, June 7, 1978, Tulsa.

16. *Tulsa City Directories* for 1919 and 1921 (Tulsa: Polk-Hoffhine Directory Com-pany, 1919 and 1921); United States Bureau of the Census, *Negroes in the United States, 1920–1932* (Washington, D.C.: Government Printing Office, 1935), 797; "The Lesson of Tulsa," *Outlook*, CXXVIII (June 15, 1921), 281; Walter F. White, "The Eruption of Tulsa," *Nation*, CXII (June 29, 1921), 909–910.

17. "Take Me Back to Tulsa," melody by Bob Wills, words by Tommy Duncan, copy-right 1941 by Peer International; copyright renewed 1968 by Mrs. Tommy [Ardith Marie] Duncan. Charles R. Townsend, *San Antonio Rose: The Life and Music of Bob Wills* (Urbana: University of Illinois Press, 1976), 207–208.

18. Interviews with W. D. Williams, June 7, 1978, Tulsa; Robert Fairchild, June 8, 1978, Tulsa; and V. H. Hodge, June 12, 1978, Tulsa; *Tulsa City Directory, 1921* (Tulsa: Polk-Hoffhine Directory Company, 1921); Mary E. Jones Parrish, *Events of the Tulsa Disaster* (n.p., n.p., n.d.), 7; Norman L. Crockett, *The Black Towns* (Lawrence, Kansas: Regents Press of Kansas, 1979), 35.

19. Interviews with W. D. Williams, June 7, 1978, Tulsa; Robert Fairchild, June 8, 1978, Tulsa; and B. E. Caruthers, July 21, 1978, Tulsa County. It may be of interest to note that whites were sometimes found in "choc" joints in black Tulsa when such places were raided by the police. Miscellaneous "Statement of Barney

Cleaver" [TS], Civil Case 1062, Oklahoma State Attorney Generals Collection, Oklahoma State Archives, Oklahoma City.

The scientific name for Choctaw root is *Apocynum cannabium*. Mitford M. Mathews (ed.), *A Dictionary of Americanisms: On Historical Principles* (Chicago: University of Chicago Press, 1951), 319. I am indebted to Dr. James R. Estes, curator of the Robert Bebb Herbarium at the University of Oklahoma, for explaining the distinction between *Apocynum cannabium* and *Cannibus sativa* (marijuana).

20. Interviews with Seymour Williams, June 2, 1978, Tulsa, and W. D. Williams, June 7, 1978, Tulsa; *Tulsa City Directory, 1921*; Parrish, *Events of the Tulsa Disaster*, 98–106; White, "The Eruption of Tulsa," 910.
21. *Tulsa City Directory, 1921*; Interviews with Henry Whitlow, June 6, 1978, Tulsa; W. D. Williams, June 7, 1978, Tulsa; and Robert Fairchild, June 8, 1978, Tulsa.
22. Interview with W. D. Williams, June 7, 1978, Tulsa; *Tulsa City Directory, 1921*.

## Chapter 2: Race Relations and Local Violence

1. John Hope Franklin, *From Slavery to Freedom: A History of Negro Americans* (4th ed.; New York: Alfred A. Knopf, 1974), 357; Richard Maxwell Brown, *Strain of Violence: Historical Studies of American Violence and Vigilantism* (New York: Oxford University Press, 1975), 324–25.
2. Of the sixty-four persons lynched in 1921, at least four were burned alive, seventeen were shot, and two were drowned. Monroe N. Work to Walter F. White, July 18, 1921, and, "Lynching Record for 1921," Administrative Files, Box C-338, National Association for the Advancement of Colored People (NAACP) Papers, Library of Congress, Washington, D.C.; Monroe N. Work (ed.), *Negro Year Book: An Annual Encyclopedia of the Negro, 1925–1926* (Tuskegee Institute, Alabama: Negro Year Book Publishing Company, 1925), 52–53.
3. Quoted in Theodore G. Vincent (ed.), *Voices of a Black Nation: Political Journalism of the Harlem Renaissance* (San Francisco: Ramparts Press, 1973), 52–53.
4. C. Vann Woodward, *The Strange Career of Jim Crow* (New York: Oxford University Press, 1957), 100–101; Marc Karson and Ronald Radosh, "The American Federation of Labor and the Negro Worker," in Julius Jacobson (ed.), *The Negro and the American Labor Movement* (Garden City, N.Y.: Doubleday and Company, 1968), 159–60; August Meier and Elliott Rudwick, *From Plantation to Ghetto* (Rev. ed.; New York: Hill and Wang, 1970), 218.
5. Sigmund Sameth, "Creek Indians: A Study of Race Relations" (M.A. thesis, University of Oklahoma, 1940), 56; Kay M. Teall (ed.), *Black History in Oklahoma: A Resource Book* (Oklahoma City: Oklahoma City Public Schools, 1971), 167–73; Edwin S. Redkey, *Black Exodus: Black Nationalist and Back-to-Africa Movements, 1890–1910* (New Haven: Yale University Press, 1969), 99–100; Nell Irvin Painter, *Exodusters: Black Migration to Kansas After Reconstruction* (New York: Alfred A. Knopf, 1977), 153, 259.
6. Teall, *Black History in Oklahoma*, 172, 202–204; William Bittle and Gilbert L. Geis, "Racial Self-Fulfillment and the Rise of an All-Negro Community in Oklahoma," in August Meier and Elliott Rudwick (eds.), *The Making of Black America* (New York: Atheneum, 1969), II, 109; interview with W. D. Williams, June 7, 1978, Tulsa.

7. New York *Age*, October 24, 1907, p.8; Arrell M. Gibson, *Oklahoma: A History of Five Centuries* (Norman, Oklahoma: Harlow Publishing Corporation, 1965), 353; Teall, *Black History in Oklahoma*, 172, 202–204, 225; Tulsa *Star*, March 30, 1918, p. 4; interview with W. D. Williams, June 7, 1978, Tulsa.

8. Work, *Negro Year Book, 1925–1926*, 309–403; National Association for the Advancement of Colored People, *Thirty Years of Lynching in the United States, 1889–1918* (New York: NAACP, 1919), 86–87, plus supplements 1–3 (1919–1921).

   Philip S. Foner, "The I.W.W. and the Black Worker," *Journal of Negro History*, LV (1970), 45–64; James Weinstein, *The Decline of Socialism in America, 1912–1925* (New York: Monthly Review Press, 1967), 68; "State Platform, Socialist Party of Oklahoma—1912," and "Negroes Favor Socialist Party" [Handbill], Oklahoma State File, Socialist Party of America (SPA) Papers, Duke University, Durham, North Carolina.

   The largest vote for the Socialist party in Tulsa was in the city election of 1912, when a Socialist candidate received 7.7 percent of the vote. There was, however, a Socialist party office in Tulsa until at least the early 1930s. James M. Mitchell, "Politics in a Boom Town: Tulsa From 1906–1930" (M.A. thesis, University of Tulsa, 1950), 56, 62, 65–66, 82, 87–93, 97, 103; W. L. Garver [Secretary, Socialist Party of Tulsa] to the *American Guardian*, January 30, 1933, Oklahoma State File, SPA Papers, Duke.

9. I. A. Newby, *Jim Crow's Defense: Anti-Negro Thought in America, 1900–1930* (Baton Rouge: Louisiana State University Press, 1965), xi–xii; John Higham, *Strangers in the Land: Patterns of American Nativism, 1860–1925* (New York: Atheneum, 1963), 271; Madison Grant, *The Passing of the Great Race, or the Racial Basis of European History* (New York: Charles Scribner's Sons, 1918), 77; Charles W. Gould, *America, A Family Matter* (New York: Charles Scribner's Sons, 1922), 125.

10. It has been estimated that between 1915 and 1944, there were some 6,000 members of the Klan in Tulsa. Charles C. Alexander, *The Ku Klux Klan in the Southwest* (Lexington: University of Kentucky Press, 1965), 43–45; Kenneth T. Jackson, *The Ku Klux Klan in the City, 1915–1930* (New York: Oxford University Press, 1967), 239. See also Marion Monteval, *The Klan Inside Out* (Claremore, Oklahoma: Monarch Publishing Company, 1924), 69.

11. Alexander, *The Ku Klux Klan in the Southwest*, 43–45, 48, 135.

12. Chicago Commission on Race Relations, *The Negro in Chicago* (Chicago: University of Chicago Press, 1922), 481, quoted in Tuttle, *Race Riot*, 209.

13. Herbert Aptheker, *Afro-American History: The Modern Era* (New York: Citadel Press, 1971), 166; Franklin, *From Slavery to Freedom*, 353; Robert T. Kerlin, *The Voice of the Negro, 1919* (1920; rpt. New York: Arno Press and the New York Times, 1968), 20.

14. Amy Jacques-Garvey (comp.), *Philosophy and Opinions of Marcus Garvey, or Africa for the Africans* (1925; rpt. New York: Arno Press and the New York Times, 1969), II, 20.

15. Kerlin, *Voice of the Negro*, 9; Meier and Rudwick, *From Plantation to Ghetto*, 222; Peter Gilbert (ed.), *The Selected Writings of John Edward Bruce: Militant Black Journalist* (New York: Arno Press and the New York Times, 1971), 158.

16. Kerlin, *Voice of the Negro*, 19.

17. Arthur I. Waskow, *From Race Riot to Sit-In, 1919 and the 1960's: A Study in the*

*Connections Between Conflict and Violence* (Garden City, N.Y.: Doubleday, 1967), p. 178.

18. Interview with W. D. Williams, June 7, 1978, Tulsa; Loren L. Gill, "The Tulsa Race Riot" (M.A. thesis, University of Tulsa, 1946), 4; NAACP Secretary to Professor Hughes, January 24, 1917, in Series I, Tulsa Branch File, Box G-175, NAACP Papers, Library of Congress; Theodore G. Vincent, *Black Power and the Garvey Movement* (San Francisco: Ramparts Press, 1972), 74–75; Vincent, *Voices of a Black Nation*, 123.

One such veteran was Seymour Williams, who later became one of Oklahoma's most renowned high school football coaches at Booker T. Washington High School in Tulsa. On the night of the race riot, Williams—who had been wounded in action in France—went out with his 45-calibre Army revolver in an attempt to stem the invasion of whites into Greenwood. He held his position throughout the night, and when morning broke, returned to his home. There, he claimed, his life was saved by his wife, who took his gun away from him when a group of whites came to their door. He had planned to meet them armed. Interview with Seymour Williams, June 2, 1978, Tulsa.

19. Tulsa *Star*, September 4, 1920, p. 4.
20. Tulsa *Times*, October 30, 1917, p. 1; Tulsa *Democrat*, October 29, 1917, pp. 1, 8; Tulsa *World*, October 30, 1917, pp. 1, 6.
21. Tulsa *Times*, October 30, 1917, p. 1.
22. Tulsa *World*, October 30, 1917, p. 1.
23. Tulsa *Times*, November 2, 1917, p. 1.
24. Tulsa *World*, October 31, 1917, p. 4.
25. H. C. Peterson and Gilbert C. Fite, *Opponents of War, 1917–1918* (Seattle: University of Washington Press, 1957), 40–41; David A. Shannon, *The Socialist Party of America: A History* (Chicago: Quadrangle Books, 1955), 106–109; Federal Writers' Project of Oklahoma, *Labor History of Oklahoma* (Oklahoma City: A. M. Van Horn, 1939), 40–42; James R. Green, *Grass-Roots Socialism: Radical Movements in the Southwest, 1895–1943* (Baton Rouge: Louisiana State University Press, 1978), 360–66.
26. Tulsa *Democrat*, November 11, 1917, p. 3; Tulsa *World*, October 31, 1917, p. 4, and November 7, 1917, p. 12.
27. Tulsa *Democrat*, November 5, p. 1, November 6, p. 5, and November 11, 1917, p. C4; Tulsa *Times*, November 6, 1917, p. 1; Tulsa *World*, October 30, p. 1, November 2, p. 1, November 3, p. 1, November 5, p. 1, and November 6, 1917, p. 1; *Tulsa City Directory, 1917* (Tulsa: Polk-Hoffhine Directory Company, 1917); National Civil Liberties Bureau, *The "Knights of Liberty" Mob and the I.W.W. Prisoners at Tulsa, Okla., November 9, 1917* (New York: National Civil Liberties Bureau, 1918), 4–5; Joyce L. Kornbluh (ed.), *Rebel Voices: An I.W.W. Anthology* (Ann Arbor: University of Michigan Press, 1964), 332–34.
28. Tulsa *World*, October 30, p. 1, November 2, p. 1, November 3, p. 1, November 5, p. 1, and November 6, 1917, p. 1; Tulsa *Democrat*, November 6, p. 5, and November 11, 1917, p. C4; Tulsa *Times*, November 6, 1917, p. 1.
29. Tulsa *World*, November 6, 1917, p. 1.
30. As for the overall political climate of Tulsa during this period, two incidents which occurred as the trial of the union men began seem relevant. On Wednesday, November 7, 1917, W. Tate Brady, "former Democratic national committee-

man from Oklahoma, heavy property owner here and Oklahoma commander of the Sons of Confederate Veterans," assaulted E. L. Fox, owner of the building where the IWW hall was located, "following an argument over the I.W.W. situation in Tulsa." And later that same day, one Tulsan shot and killed another in the streets over a violent argument which their wives had had over the European war. Tulsa *World*, November 7, pp. 8, 12, and November 9, 1917, p. 16; Tulsa *Times*, November 8, 1917, pp. 1, 2, 6; Tulsa *Democrat*, November 7, 1917, p. 1.

31. Tulsa *World*, November 6, p. 1, and November 7, 1917, p. 8; Tulsa *Democrat*, November 7, 1917, p. 1; Tulsa *Times*, November 8, 1917, p. 1.

32. Tulsa *World*, November 9, 1917, p. 3; Tulsa *Times*, November 9, 1917, p. 5.

33. Elsewhere in the same editorial, the *World* stated that anyone trying to decrease the supply of oil "for one-hundreth of a second is a traitor and ought to be shot!" Tulsa *World*, November 9, 1917, pp. 3, 4.

   The authorship of this unsigned editorial is unclear. Eugene Lorton was at the time the "senior" editor of the *World*, and Glenn H. Condon was the newspaper's managing editor. In its pamphlet on the incident, the National Civil Liberties Bureau [NCLB] made the following assertion in regards to the editorial: "It may be interesting to note that the editor of the Tulsa World, Glenn Conlin [*sic*], who personally wrote this, attended all the trials, and that he and his wife were witnesses to the whipping, tarring and feathering, having gone along in the automobile as spectators," NCLB, *The "Knights of Liberty" Mob*, 10. Yet, regardless of the question of the authorship of the editorial, it would appear that the *World's* pro-vigilante, pro-terrorism stance against Tulsans who opposed the war was approved, if not actually fostered, by Lorton.

   Although "Get Out the Hemp" was undoubtedly the acme of the *World's* rabid, wartime sensationalism, it should not be assumed that the newspaper directed its venom only against political radicals and union men during this period. For example, Tulsa was at this time involved in a Liberty Bond campaign, and two days after the Pew bombing the *World* published a front-page story about a local launderer who would not purchase any bonds, entitled "Say Laundry Man Is Unpatriotic." The story listed the man's name and place of employment, predicting that he "may be in serious trouble before nightfall." Tulsa *World*, October 31, 1917, p. 1.

34. Tulsa *World*, November 10, 1917, pp. 1, 2; Blanche Riehn [?] to "Dear Comrade"—with note on back signed by Frank Ryan—October 10, 1914, Oklahoma State File, SPA Papers, Duke.

35. Tulsa *Democrat*, November 10, 1917, p. 1; Tulsa *World*, November 10, 1917, pp. 1, 2; Tulsa *Times*, November 10, 1917, p. 1.

36. Tulsa *Democrat*, November 10, 1917, pp. 1, 8; Tulsa *World*, November 10, 1917, p. 1; Tulsa *Times*, November 9, p. 1, and November 10, 1917, p. 1; NCLB, *The "Knights of Liberty" Mob*, 6–7.

37. A *Times* reporter stated that the "Knights of Liberty," garbed as Ku Klux Klansmen, "presented a picturesque scene." Tulsa *Times*, November 10, 1917, p. 1; Tulsa *World*, November 10, 1917, p. 1; Tulsa *Democrat*, November 10, 1917, p. 1; NCLB, *The "Knights of Liberty" Mob*, 7.

38. Tulsa *Democrat*, November 10, 1917, p. 1; Tulsa *Times*, November 10, 1917, p. 1; Tulsa *World*, November 10, 1917, p. 1; NCLB, *The "Knights of Liberty" Mob*, 7–8, 13.

39. In the version of this statement reprinted in Kornbluh, *Rebel Voices,* 334, the detective is "named Blaine." Tulsa *Democrat,* November 10, 1917, p. 1; Tulsa *Times,* November 9, p. 1, and November 10, 1917, p. 1; Tulsa *World,* November 10, 1917, p. 1; NCLB, *The "Knights of Liberty" Mob,* 8–9.
40. NCLB, *The "Knights of Liberty" Mob,* 13–14.
41. Tulsa *World,* November 10, p. 1, and November 11, 1917, p. 1; Tulsa *Democrat,* November 10, p. 8, and November 11, 1917, p. 1; Tulsa *Times,* November 10, p. 6, and November 12, 1917, p. 7; NCLB, *The "Knights of Liberty" Mob,* 15–16.
42. Tulsa *World,* November 12, p. 4, and November 13, 1917, p. 4; Oklahoma *World,* November 22, 1917, p. 1; Tulsa *Democrat,* November 11, 1917, p. 3; NCLB, *The "Knights of Liberty" Mob,* 15–16.

    In December, 1917, Charles Krieger, a Tulsan, was arrested for bombing the Pew home. He was acquitted, owing to flimsy evidence and what appears to have been a fair-minded judge, but not until May, 1920—nearly two and one-half years after the bombing. Historians H. C. Peterson and Gilbert Fite wrote about Krieger: "It seems that he was luckier than many other I.W.W.'s because of the fairmindedness and impartiality of Judge R. S. Cole. Some judges refused to bow to the popular hysteria. In Oklahoma and elsewhere, however, there was a general state of mind reminiscent of the attitude of King James I, who said about the Puritans, 'I will make them conform or I will harry them out of the land,'" *Opponents of War,* 176. On this incident see also William T. Lampe (comp.), *Tulsa County in the World War* (Tulsa: Tulsa County Historical Society, 1919), 221–22.
43. That all of the defendants were white is based on two sources of evidence. First, city directories for Tulsa during this period listed a person's race, in addition to his name, home address, and occupation. Of those defendants whose names were included in the *Tulsa City Directory, 1917,* all were designated as white. Secondly, owing to the nature of their reporting during this period, it is simply inconceivable that either the *World,* the *Times,* or the *Democrat* would have failed to mention it if any of the defendants had been black, if any were. [None of the extant copies of Tulsa's various black newspapers carried any material about this incident.]
44. Tulsa *World,* March 18, 1919, p. 1; Tulsa *Times,* March 18, 1919, p. 1; Tulsa *Democrat,* March 18, 1919, p. 1.
45. Tulsa *Democrat,* March 18, 1919, p. 1; Tulsa *World,* March 18, 1919, p. 1; Tulsa *Times,* March 18, 1919, p. 1. Unfortunately, no copies of the Tulsa *Star,* the city's black newspaper, for March or April of 1919 could be located.
46. Tulsa *Democrat,* March 19, p. 11, March 20, p. 9, and March 21, 1919, pp. 10, 16; Tulsa *Times,* March 20, p. 1, March 21, p. 1, and March 22, 1919, p. 3; Tulsa *World,* March 21, 1919, p. 1. There is some evidence that blacks visited the courthouse twice. See Tulsa *Times,* March 22, 1919, p. 3.
47. Tulsa *Democrat,* March 21, 1919, p. 16.
48. Tulsa *World,* March 23, p. 1, March 24, p. 11, March 25, p. 15, and March 26, 1919, p. 3.
49. Tulsa *Times,* March 22, 1919, p. 3. The author located no evidence to support or contradict Abernathy's "class analysis" of the group of blacks that went down to the city jail on the night of March 13, 1919. Two years later, however, when a similar situation developed in the case of Dick Rowland, "wealthy" blacks were included in the group that went down to the county courthouse after rumors of a

possible lynching attempt were heard on the city's streets. Interview with W. D. Williams, June 7, 1978, Tulsa.

50. Tulsa *World*, August 22, p. 1, and August 24, 1920, p. 1; Tulsa *Tribune*, August 22, p. 1, August 25, p. 1, August 27, p. 1, and August 28, 1920, p. 1.

51. Tulsa *World*, August 22, p. 1, and August 24, 1920, p. 1; Tulsa *Tribune*, August 22, p. 1, August 24, pp. 1, 4, and August 28, 1920, p. 1.

52. Tulsa *World*, August 22, p. 1, and August 24, 1920, p. 1. Tulsa *Tribune*, August 22, p. 1, August 24, pp. 1, 4, and August 25, 1920, p. 1. See also Tulsa *Star*, August 28, 1920, p. 1

53. Tulsa *World*, August 27, 1920, p. 1; Tulsa *Tribune*, August 28, 1920, p. 3. See also Tulsa *World*, August 22, p. 1, August 23, p. 10, August 24, p. 1, August 25, pp. 1, 12, and August 28, 1920, p. 1; Tulsa *Tribune*, August 22, p. 1, August 23, p. 1, August 24, pp. 1, 4, August 25, p. 1, August 27, 1920, p. 1; Tulsa *Star*, August 28, 1920, p. 1. The Tulsa *Times* had folded, and the *Tribune* was the successor to the *Democrat*.

54. For one week after the Nida shooting, Roy Belton was identified in the newspapers as "T. M. Owens," which may have been an alias which he gave to the police. His age was also given as seventeen and nineteen. Tulsa *World*, August 22, p. 1, August 24, p. 1, August 29, p. 9, September 1, p. 12, and September 2, 1920, p. 9; Tulsa *Tribune*, August 23, p. 1, August 24, p. 1, and August 28, 1920, p. 1.

55. Tulsa *Tribune*, August 23, p. 1, August 24, p. 1, and August 27, 1920, p. 1; Tulsa *World*, August 24, p. 1, and September 2, 1920, p. 1.

56. Tulsa *Tribune*, August 25, p. 1, and August 27, 1920, p. 1; Tulsa *World*, August 25, pp. 1, 12, August 28, pp. 1, 9, August 29, p. 9, August 30, p. 1, and September 2, 1920, p. 1.

57. The jail was located on the top floor of the building, and, in a situation that was to be repeated the next year, the Sheriff ordered that the elevator be sent to the top floor each night. Tulsa *World*, August 25, p. 12, and August 31, 1920, p. 4; Tulsa *Tribune*, August 28, 1920, p. 1.

58. Tulsa *Tribune*, August 27, 1920, p. 1; Tulsa *World*, August 28, 1920, p. 1.

59. Raymond Sharp said that he did not know how to plea, and the not-guilty plea was entered for him. Tulsa *Tribune*, August 28, 1920, p. 1; Tulsa *World*, August 28, pp. 1, 9, and August 29, 1920, p. 9.

60. Tulsa *World*, August 29, p. 1, and August 30, 1920, p. 3; Tulsa *Tribune*, August 29, 1920, pp. 1–2.

61. After Roy Belton was abducted, Sheriff Woolley took Harmon and Sharp by automobile to the jail in Muskogee. Tulsa *World*, August 29, p. 1, and August 30, 1920, pp. 1–3; Tulsa *Tribune*, August 29, 1920, pp. 1–2.

62. The crowd that viewed the lynching was estimated at two thousand people and higher. Tulsa *World*, August 30, 1920, pp. 1–3; Tulsa *Tribune*, August 29, 1920, p. 1; Tulsa *Star*, September 4, 1920, p. 1; White, "The Eruption of Tulsa," 909.

63. Tulsa *World*, August 29, p. 1, and August 30, 1920, p. 1; Tulsa *Tribune*, August 29, 1920, p. 1.

64. Tulsa *Tribune*, August 29, 1920, p. 2.

65. Tulsa *World*, August 29, 1920, p. 1.

66. *Ibid.*; Tulsa *Tribune*, August 29, 1920, p. 3. A collection of clippings about this incident are located in the Administrative Files, Box C-364 [Lynching—Oklahoma], NAACP Papers, Library of Congress.

67. Gustafson's and Woolley's statements on the lynching were almost identical. Tulsa *World*, August 30, 1920, pp. 1–3.

68. Tulsa *World*, August 30, p. 4, August 31, pp. 1, 4, September 1, pp. 1, 4, 12, September 2, pp. 1, 4, September 3, pp. 1, 18, September 5, p. A1, September 6, p. 1, and September 10, 1920, pp. 1, 13; Tulsa *Tribune*, August 31, p. 12, September 6, p. 1, September 9, p. 1, September 10, p. 1, September 21, p. 2, September 24, p. 1, and September 29, 1920, p. 1.
69. Tulsa *Star*, September 4, 1920, pp. 1, 4.

## Chapter 3: Race Riot

1. Interviews with W. D. Williams, June 7, 1978, Tulsa, and Robert Fairchild, June 8, 1978, Tulsa; *Tulsa City Directory, 1921* (Tulsa: Polk-Hoffhine Directory Company, 1921); "Alumni Roster" for Booker T. Washington High School, 1916–1929, courtesy of W. D. Williams.
2. Interviews with W. D. Williams, June 7, 1978, Tulsa, and Robert Fairchild, June 8, 1978, Tulsa; Tulsa *Tribune*, May 31, 1921 [incorrectly cited as June 1, 1921], in Loren L. Gill, "The Tulsa Race Riot" (M.A. thesis, University of Tulsa, 1946), 22.
3. Walter White wrote in the New York *Evening Post*: "The immediate cause of the riot was a white girl who claimed that Dick Rowland, a colored youth of nineteen, attempted to assault her. . . . The following day the Tulsa *Tribune* told of the charge and the arrest of Rowland. Chief of Police John A. Gustafson, Sheriff McCullough, Mayor T. D. Evans, and a number of reputable citizens, among them a prominent oil operator, all declared that the girl had not been molested; that no attempt at criminal assault had been made. Victor F. Barnett, managing editor of the *Tribune* stated that his paper had since learned that the original story that the girl's face was scratched and her clothes torn was untrue," quoted in "Mob Fury and Race Hatred as a National Danger," *Literary Digest*, LXIX (June 18, 1921), 8; Tulsa *World*, June 2, 1921, p. 2; Mary E. Jones Parrish, *Events of the Tulsa Disaster* (n.p., n.p., n.d.), 7, 29.
4. Tulsa *World*, June 2, 1921, pp. 1–5; Interviews with W. D. Williams, June 7, 1978, Tulsa, and Robert Fairchild, June 8, 1978, Tulsa; Walter White, "The Eruption of Tulsa," *Nation*, CXII (June 29, 1921), 909. Tulsa police reports for this period no longer exist.
5. Tulsa *Tribune*, May 31, 1921, in Gill, "The Tulsa Race Riot," 21–22. In his narrative, Loren Gill properly identified this article as being in the May 31, 1921 issue of the *Tribune*, but incorrectly footnotes it as being in the June 1 issue. The inference is clear that Gill, who has since passed away, did not have a complete copy of the May 31 issue of the *Tribune* to work with, but merely this article.
6. Interview with W. D. Williams, June 7, 1978, Tulsa. The Thompson statement is in Parrish, *Events of the Tulsa Disaster*, 29–30.
7. Statement of "A.H." in Parrish, *Events of the Tulsa Disaster*, 47–49.
8. Charles F. Barrett, *Oklahoma after Fifty Years: A History of the Sooner State and Its People, 1889–1939* (Hopkinsville, Kentucky: Historical Record Association, 1941), 206. Ross T. Warner wrote: "A nineteen-year-old Negro youth allegedly attacked a white girl elevator operator in the Drexel Building. This incident was played up sensationally in the evening papers, and the talk of lynching spread like prairie fire," *Oklahoma Boy: An Autobiography* (n.p., n.p., n.d.), 136.
9. Tulsa *Tribune*, May 31, 1921, in Gill, "The Tulsa Race Riot," 22. Miscellaneous statement of Bill McCullough [TS], Civil Case 1062, Box 25, Oklahoma State Attorney Generals Collection, Oklahoma State Archives (OSA), Oklahoma City; R.

Halliburton, "The Tulsa Race War of 1921," *Journal of Black Studies*, XX (March, 1972), 337; White, "Eruption of Tulsa," 910.

10. Tulsa *Tribune*, June 3, p. 1; and June 6, 1921, p. 3.

11. Tulsa *Tribune*, June 6, 1921, p. 3; "Message [of] Mayor to Commissioners," Record of Commission Proceedings, City of Tulsa, Vol. XV, June 14, 1921, p. 25, in the City Commission Secretary's Office, City Hall, Tulsa; Clipping File for lynchings in Oklahoma, Administrative Files, Box C-364, NAACP Papers, Library of Congress; Interviews with W. D. Williams, June 7, 1978, Tulsa, and Robert Fairchild, June 8, 1978, Tulsa.

A few years before the Tulsa riot, blacks armed with high-powered rifles had hidden within range of the jail in Muskogee where an accused black was held, and where a crowd of whites had gathered. Trouble was averted when the whites were dispersed by the authorities; the blacks went home. And less than four months after the Tulsa race riot, Oklahoma City barely escaped having a similar racial clash after a group of whites had taken a young black from the county jail and lynched him outside of the capital city. Joseph B. Thoburn and Muriel H. Wright, *Oklahoma, A History of the Sooner State and Its People* (New York: Lewis Historical Publishing Company, 1929), II, 291.

12. Tulsa *Tribune*, June 3, 1921, p. 1; Tulsa *World*, June 10, 1921, p. 8; Statement of O. W. Gurley, *State of Oklahoma* v. *Will Robinson, et al.*, Oklahoma State Attorney Generals Collection, Oklahoma State Archives, Oklahoma City.

13. Interviews with Seymour Williams, June 2, 1978, Tulsa; W. D. Williams, June 7, 1978, Tulsa; and Robert Fairchild, June 8, 1978, Tulsa; statements of Henry Jacobs and John Henry Potts, Civil Case 1062, Oklahoma State Attorney Generals Collection, Oklahoma State Archives; White, "The Eruption of Tulsa," 910; San Francisco *Chronicle*, June 4, 1921, p. 3; Tulsa *World*, June 2, p. 7, June 3, p. 1, June 6, p. 3, June 9, p. 4, June 10, p. 8, July 4, pp. 1, 2, July 15, p. 1, July 20, pp. 1, 7, and July 21, 1921, p. 3.

14. Major Jas. A. Bell ["Report on Activities of the National Guard on the Night of May 31st and June 1st, 1921"] to Lt. Col. L. J. F. Rooney, July 2, 1921, in the Governor James B. A. Robertson Papers [hereafter cited as the "Robertson Papers"], Oklahoma State Archives. See also Redmond S. Cole to Jas. G. Findlay, June 6, 1921, in the Redmond S. Cole Papers, Western History Collection, University of Oklahoma, Norman.

15. Bell to Rooney, July 2, 1921, in Robertson Papers, Oklahoma State Archives.

16. Interview with I. S. Pittman, July 28, 1978, Tulsa; Tulsa *Tribune*, July 3, 1921, p. 1.

17. Interview with Robert Fairchild, June 8, 1978, Tulsa; Tulsa *Tribune*, June 3, 1921, p. 1; Tulsa *World*, July 7, 1921, p. 3; White, "Eruption of Tulsa," 910; Frances W. Prentice, "Oklahoma Race Riot," *Scribner's*, XC (August, 1931), 151–57.

18. Major Byron Kirkpatrick ["Activities on the Night of May 31, 1921 at Tulsa, Okla."] to Lt. Col. L. J. F. Rooney, July 1, 1921, and, Bell to Rooney, July 2, 1921, in Robertson Papers, Oklahoma State Archives; Barrett, *Oklahoma after Fifty Years*, 207–209.

19. Telegram, John A. Gustafson, Wm. McCullough, and V. W. Biddison to Governor J. B. A. Robertson, June 1, 1921, and, Kirkpatrick to Rooney, July 1, 1921, in Robertson Papers; Barrett, *Oklahoma after Fifty Years*, 209–12.

20. Citing an interview that he conducted with George Henry Blaine on June 5, 1946, Loren Gill stated that about five hundred "armed men and boys" were given spe-

cial commissions by the police within one-half hour after the outbreak of violence, "The Tulsa Race Riot," 28; Tulsa *World*, June 10, 1921, p. 8; interview with Seymour Williams, June 2, 1978, Tulsa.

21. Barrett, *Oklahoma after Fifty Years*, 210–11; Statement of Mr. [S.J.?] McGee, Civil Case 1062, Oklahoma State Attorney Generals Collection, Oklahoma State Archives; Tulsa *World*, June 2, 1921, p. 2.

22. Statement of Major C. W. Daly, Civil Case 1062, Oklahoma State Attorney Generals Collection, Oklahoma State Archives; Interviews with Seymour Williams, June 2, 1978, Tulsa, W. D. Williams, June 7, 1978, Tulsa, Henry Whitlow, June 6, 1978, Tulsa, V. H. Hodge, June 12, 1978, Tulsa, N. C. Williams, July 20, 1978, Tulsa, and B. E. Caruthers, July 21, 1978, Tulsa County.

23. Tulsa *Tribune*, June 3, 1921, p. 1; Tulsa *World*, June 2, 1921, p. 2; Ed Wheeler, "Profile of a Race Riot," *Oklahoma Impact Magazine*, IV (June–July, 1971), 21; interview with W. D. Williams, June 7, 1978, Tulsa.

24. Tulsa *Tribune*, June 5, 1921, 7; Tulsa *World*, July 19, 1921, p. 7.

25. Interviews with W. D. Williams, June 7, 1978, Tulsa, Robert Fairchild, June 8, 1978, Tulsa, N. C. Williams, July 20, 1978, Tulsa, and I. S. Pittman, July 28, 1978, Tulsa; Tulsa *Tribune*, July 15, 1921, p. 9.

26. Tulsa *Tribune*, June 1, 1921, p. 6; Tulsa *World*, June 2, 1921, pp. 1, 7; interview with Robert Fairchild, June 8, 1978, Tulsa. Some whites later claimed that the Mt. Zion Church had been used as an arsenal by blacks, as a way to rationalize its destruction. W. D. Williams, however, has provided us with a bit of compelling evidence to relegate such an assertion into oblivion. On a Sunday morning shortly before the riot, Williams and some of his friends had crawled throughout the structure—probably in an attempt to avoid the church service—and saw no arms or ammunition. Interview with W. D. Williams, June 7, 1978, Tulsa. See also Gill, "The Tulsa Race Riot," 32–33, 35n.

27. White, "Eruption of Tulsa," 910; New York *Times*, June 2, 1921, pp. 1–2; Tulsa *World*, July 14, 1921, p. 1; Wheeler, "Profile of a Race Riot," 22; interviews with Seymour Williams, June 2, 1978, Tulsa, W. D. Williams, June 7, 1978, and Robert Fairchild, June 8, 1978, Tulsa.

28. Tulsa *World*, June 2, 1921, p. 1; Captain Frank Van Voorhis ["Detailed Report of Negro Uprising for Service Company, 3rd Infantry, Oklahoma National Guard"] to Lieutenant Colonel L. J. F. Rooney, July 30, 1921, in Robertson Papers, Oklahoma State Archives; interviews with Seymour Williams, June 2, 1978, Tulsa, W. D. Williams, June 7, 1978, Tulsa, Robert Fairchild, June 8, 1978, Tulsa, V. H. Hodge, June 12, 1978, Tulsa, and I. S. Pittman, July 28, 1978, Tulsa.

29. Tulsa *Tribune*, June 3, 1921, p. 7.

30. Barrett, *Oklahoma after Fifty Years*, 211–12; Tulsa *Tribune*, June 3, 1921, p. 1; interview with Henry Whitlow, June 6, 1978, Tulsa; Warner, *Oklahoma Boy*, 138; Parrish, *Events of the Tulsa Disaster*, 11.

31. Prentice, "Oklahoma Race Riot," 155; Barrett, *Oklahoma after Fifty Years*, 213.

32. Barrett, *Oklahoma after Fifty Years*, 213–14; Tulsa *World*, June 2, p. 2, June 3, p. 2, and July 21, 1921, p. 3.

33. Tulsa *World*, June 2, p. 2, July 14, 1921, p. 2; Oklahoma City *Daily Oklahoman*, June 5, 1921, p. 4; Halliburton, "The Tulsa Race War of 1921," 343.

34. Parrish, *Events of the Tulsa Disaster*, 9–12; Theodore G. Vincent, *Black Power and the Garvey Movement* (San Francisco: Ramparts Press, 1972), 75, 146–47.

35. New York *Times*, June 2, 1921, p. 2; Clarence B. Douglas, *The History of Tulsa, Oklahoma: A City with a Personality* (Chicago: S. J. Clarke Publishing Company, 1921), II, 621.

36. Tulsa *Tribune*, June 2, 1971 [*sic*], p. A7; New York *Times*, June 2, pp. 1–2, and June 8, 1921, p. 7.

37. Bell to Rooney, July 2, 1921, and Major Paul R. Brown to Adjutant General Barrett, July 1, 1921, in Robertson Papers.

38. Gill, "The Tulsa Race Riot," 48–49, 67.

39. *Ibid.*, 67.

40. Record of Commission Proceedings, City of Tulsa, September 27, p. 299, July 26, p. 133, July 29, p. 152, September 23, p. 283, and October 14, 1921, p. 356.

41. Barrett, *Oklahoma after Fifty Years*, 216.

42. White, "The Eruption of Tulsa," 910.

43. Warner, *Oklahoma Boy*, 137–38; interview with Henry Whitlow, June 6, 1978, Tulsa; Calvin Chase, "A Report From the Tulsa Riot Scene," Washington *Bee*, June 11, 1921, in Vincent, *Voices of a Black Nation*, 51–52 (See also White, "The Eruption of Tulsa," 910); Gill, "The Tulsa Race Riot," 46. Gill cites interviews which he conducted in the 1940s with Police Commissioner J. M. Adkison, Police Captain George H. Blaine, and Dr. George H. Miller.

44. Gill, "The Tulsa Race Riot," 45–46.

45. Interview with W. D. Williams, June 7, 1978, Tulsa; Oklahoma City *Black Dispatch*, June 10, 1921, in Teall, *Black History in Oklahoma*, 208.

46. Gill, "The Tulsa Race Riot," 47, 49, 50, 78–79. A different estimate, that of 860 homes and stores having been burned, is to be found in Douglas, *The History of Tulsa*, II, 621.

47. Record of Commission Proceedings, City of Tulsa, June 14, 1921, to June 6, 1922. The secretary of the City Commission did not record all of the claims presented to the commission in the Record; in the minutes for the July 29, 1921, meeting, a long list of claimants and claims is concluded with the notation, "and others see list on file" (p. 151), but I could not locate this file.

48. Gill, "The Tulsa Race Riot," 55.

49. *Ibid.*, 49–51; Record of Commission Proceedings, City of Tulsa, July 26, p. 142, and July 29, 1921, p. 151.

50. Gill, "The Tulsa Race Riot," 71.

## Chapter 4: Law, Order, and the Politics of Relief

1. Mary E. Jones Parrish, *Events of the Tulsa Disaster* (n.p., n.p., n.d.), 224–25; interview with Seymour Williams, June 2, 1978, Tulsa; Tulsa *World*, June 1, pp. 1–3, and June 2, 1921, p. 1; Tulsa *Tribune*, June 1, pp. 1–2, June 2, p. 1, and June 7, 1921, p. 4.

2. Citizens Security Bank and Trust Company, *Ad Libs to Bixby History, 1924–1974* (n.p., n.p., n.d.), 61; interviews with W. D. Williams, June 7, 1978, Tulsa, and Robert Fairchild, June 8, 1978, Tulsa; Clarence B. Douglas, *The History of Tulsa, Oklahoma: A City with a Personality* (Chicago: S. J. Clarke Publishing Co., 1921), I, 623; Parrish, *Events of the Tulsa Disaster*, 13–14, 37; Loren L. Gill, "The Tulsa Race Riot," (M.A. thesis, University of Tulsa, 1946), 60, 67; Major Paul R. Brown to the Adjutant General of Oklahoma, July 1, 1921, Robertson Papers, Oklahoma State Archives; Tulsa *World*, June 3, 1921, p. 4.

3. Tulsa *World*, June 3, p. 8, and June 6, 1921, p. 9; Tulsa *Tribune*, June 3, p. 1, and June 12, 1921, p. 13; Parrish, *Events of the Tulsa Disaster*, 30–35, 43–47; Frances W. Prentice, "Oklahoma Race Riot," *Scribner's*, XC (August, 1931), 156; Gill, "The Tulsa Race Riot," 57, 64, 66. Gill also reported that some whites secured the release of blacks who were not employed by them (p. 57).

4. Minutes of Directors Meetings, Tulsa Chamber of Commerce, October 7, 1921, in the offices of the Metropolitan Tulsa Chamber of Commerce, Tulsa; Parrish, *Events of the Tulsa Disaster*, 14; Tulsa *Tribune*, June 8, 1921, p. 1; Tulsa *World*, June 2, pp. 1–2, June 3, pp. 1–2, June 4, p. 1, June 5, pp. 1–3, June 7, p. 9, and June 14, 1921, p. 16.

5. Tulsa *World*, June 9, 1921, p. 7; Parrish, *Events of the Tulsa Disaster*, 18; Halliburton, *The Tulsa Race War of 1921*, 31; Gill, "The Tulsa Race Riot," 60; Douglas, *The History of Tulsa*, I, 627; Minutes of Directors Meetings, Tulsa Chamber of Commerce, October 7, 1921.

6. Interview with Robert Fairchild, June 8, 1978, Tulsa; Gill, "The Tulsa Race Riot," 71; New York *Times*, June 2, 1921, p. 1; Tulsa *Tribune*, June 1, 1921, p. 1; Tulsa *World*, June 2, p. 7, June 3, pp. 1, 13, June 9, p. 13, and June 15, 1921, p. 16.

7. Charles F. Barrett, *Oklahoma after Fifty Years: A History of the Sooner State and Its People, 1889–1939* (Hopkinsville, Ky.: Historical Record Association, 1941), 213; Douglas, *The History of Tulsa*, I, 621–22; Captain Frank Van Voorhis to Lt. Col. L. J. F. Rooney, July 30, 1921, in Robertson Papers, Oklahoma State Archives; Tulsa *World*, June 1, pp. 1–3, June 2, p. 7, June 3, pp. 1, 13, June 4, pp. 1, 2, June 9, p. 13, and June 15, 1921, p. 16.

8. Tulsa *Tribune*, June 2, p. 10, and June 10, 1921, p. 1; Barrett, *Oklahoma after Fifty Years*, 215–16. Barrett listed only Field Orders No. 1–4 and 7. See also Tulsa *World*, June 4, 1921, pp. 1, 2.

9. Barrett, *Oklahoma after Fifty Years*, 215, 217; Tulsa *Tribune*, June 2, 1921, p. 10; Tulsa *World*, June 4, 1921, p. 1.

10. Tulsa *World*, June 6, 1921, p. 2.

11. Tulsa *Tribune*, June 3, 1921, p. 1; Barrett, *Oklahoma after Fifty Years*, 215, 217.

12. Minutes of Directors' Meetings, Tulsa Chamber of Commerce, June 3, 1921, p. 148; Tulsa *Tribune*, June 3, p. 1, June 6, p. 3, and June 9, 1921, p. 11.

13. Parrish, *Events of the Tulsa Disaster*, 20, 35–36. The term "Home Guards" presents something of a problem for the student of the riot. In its proper usage, it refers to the civilian citizen defense organization organized in Tulsa—and elsewhere—in 1917 in response to the American entry in World War I, and not to the local National Guard units. Some evidence indicates that many of these "Home Guards" were "special deputies" during the riot. Interview with W. D. Williams, June 7, 1978, Tulsa. On the formation of the Tulsa "Home Guards," see Tulsa *Democrat*, November 2, p. 1, and November 3, 1917, p. 1; Tulsa *Times*, October 31, 1917, p. 1; and Tulsa *World*, November 3, 1917, p. 3. On the Inter-Racial Committee, see *Harlow's Weekly*, December 10, 1920, p. 15; Tulsa *Star*, November 27, 1920, pp. 1, 8; and January 1, 1921, p. 2; and Tulsa *Tribune*, June 23, 1921, p. 5.

14. During the period under martial law, the legally sanctioned forces of "law and order" in Tulsa included the National Guard, the local police and sheriff's forces, some three hundred uniformed veterans under the local American Legion post commander, and—for a short period—those men who were given special police commissions on the night of the riot. Douglas, *The History of Tulsa*, I, 623–24,

627; Tulsa *Tribune*, June 2, p. 1, June 6, p. 1, and June 17, 1921, p. 2; Tulsa *World*, June 3, p. 1, June 4, pp. 1, 2, 15, June 6, p. 1, and June 9, 1921, p. 11.

15. Tulsa *Tribune*, June 2, 1971 [sic], p. A7; Tulsa *World*, June 2, p. 1, June 3, p. 8, June 4, p. 4, June 6, p. 7, June 7, p. 7, and June 9, 1921, p. 9.

16. Bell to Rooney, July 2, 1921, in Robertson Papers, Oklahoma State Archives; Douglas, *The History of Tulsa*, I, 627; Gill, "The Tulsa Race Riot," 59n, 62, 66; Tulsa *World*, June 3, 1921, p. 9; Oklahoma City *Daily Oklahoman*, June 5, 1921, p. 4.

17. Oklahoma *Sun*, August 3, 1921, p. 3; Parrish, *Events of the Tulsa Disaster*, 14–20, 24–27; Tulsa *World*, June 2, p. 7, June 10, pp. 7, 20, and June 24, 1921, p. 3.

18. Tulsa *Tribune*, June 2, p. 1, June 4, 1921, pp. 1, 6; Tulsa *World*, June 2, p. 7, June 3, p. 1, June 4, p. 1, June 7, pp. 1, 7, June 9, p. 8, and June 30, 1921, p. 14; Parrish, *Events of the Tulsa Disaster*, 20; Douglas, *The History of Tulsa*, I, 623.

19. Interviews with Seymour Williams, June 2, 1978, Tulsa, W. D. Williams, June 7, 1978, Tulsa, and V. H. Hodge, June 12, 1978, Tulsa; Tulsa *World*, June 6, pp. 9, 10, June 7, pp. 1, 2, June 8, pp. 2, 7, 15, and December 24, 1921, p. 9; Parrish, *Events of the Tulsa Disaster*, 20.

20. Tulsa *World*, June 9, p. 1, June 12, p. 4, and June 15, 1921, P. 12; Oklahoma City *Daily Oklahoman*, June 3, 1921, p. 16; Administrative Files, Series F—"Tulsa, Oklahoma Riot Fund," Box C-162, NAACP Papers, Library of Congress.

21. Minutes of Directors' Meetings, Tulsa Chamber of Commerce, June 15, 1921, p. 154.

22. *Ibid.*, June 2, 1921, pp. 146–47.

23. "The Tulsa Race Riots," *Independent*, CV (June 18, 1921), 647.

24. Tulsa *World*, June 4, p. 3, June 5, p. 1, and June 16, 1921, p. 3; Gill, "The Tulsa Race Riot," p. 69.

25. In the end, however, it appears that the Executive Welfare Committee did turn over some $26,000 which it had accumulated to the Red Cross. The Tulsa *World* also raised some $5,600 for relief work. Tulsa *World*, June 3, pp. 1, 8, June 4, pp. 3, 9, 13, June 9, p. 9, June 13, p. 4, June 15, p. 4, June 16, p. 3, and June 1, 1921, p. 8; Douglas, *The History of Tulsa*, I, 623; Walter White to J. A. O. Preus, October 25, 1921, Civil Case 1062, Oklahoma State Attorney Generals Collection, Oklahoma State Archives; Gill, "The Tulsa Race Riot," 68–69; Tulsa *Tribune*, June 11, 1921, p. 2.

26. Record of Commission Proceedings, City of Tulsa, June 14, 1921, pp. 24–26; Minutes of Directors' Meetings, Tulsa Chamber of Commerce, June 15, 1921, pp. 154–56; Tulsa *World*, June 15, pp. 1, 7, and June 16, 1921, pp. 1, 2; Tulsa *Tribune*, June 14, pp. 1, 2, and June 15, 1921, pp. 1, 11.

27. Tulsa *Tribune*, June 3, p. 1, June 19, p. 1, and June 29, 1921, p. 5; Tulsa *World*, June 3, p. 1, June 6, p. 2, June 24, p. 2, June 29, p. 16, July 8, p. 9, and July 29, 1921, p. 3; Douglas, *The History of Tulsa*, I, 624.

28. Fire Ordinance No. 2156 affected white property owners in the burned district as well. Tulsa *World*, June 8, p. 2, June 10, p. 17, and July 10, 1921, p. 17; Tulsa *Tribune*, June 7, 1921, p. 1; White to Preus, October 25, 1921, in Oklahoma State Attorney Generals Collection, Oklahoma State Archives.

29. Record of Commission Proceedings, City of Tulsa, June 14, 1921, p. 25; Tulsa *World*, June 15, 1921, pp. 1, 7.

30. Minutes of Directors' Meetings, Tulsa Chamber of Commerce, July 1, p. 162, July

15, p. 171, July 18, pp. 173–74, July 19, p. 175, and, July 22, 1921, no pagination.

31. Minutes of Directors' Meetings, Tulsa Chamber of Commerce, August 19, 1921, p. 204.

32. Record of Commission Proceedings, City of Tulsa, June 28, p. 63, and August 26, 1921, pp. 231–33. During the August 26 meeting, the City Commission passed Fire Ordinance 2182, which was said to be "especially repealing ordinance no. 2156," *ibid.*, p. 233. The author was unable, however, to detect any really significant difference between the two as they affected black Tulsa, as published in the Tulsa *World*: June 10, 11, 12, August 30, 31, and September 1, 1921. *Tulsa City Directory, 1921* (Tulsa: Polk-Hoffhine Directory Co., 1921).

33. Parrish, *Events of the Tulsa Disaster*, 20; Tulsa *World*, June 23, 1921, p. 16; Tulsa *Tribune*, June 9, p. 3, and June 19, 1921, p. 1.

34. Tulsa *World*, August 15, p. 1, August 26, p. 3, and September 2, 1921, p. 1; Tulsa *Tribune*, March 19, 1959, p. 41; interview with Mrs. Mozella Jones, June 20, 1978, Tulsa.

35. Record of Commission Proceedings, City of Tulsa, June 14, 1921, pp. 23–26.

36. The Reconstruction Committee appointed some nine sub-committees to "help" black Tulsans, including an "industrial and railroads" sub-committee; what these groups did, if anything, could not be determined. Tulsa *World*, June 17, p. 7, June 18, p. 14, June 23, p. 16, and June 25, 1921, p. 16; Tulsa *Tribune*, June 27, 1921, p. 5; Record of Commission Proceedings, City of Tulsa, June 29, pp. 68–69, June 30, pp. 70–71, July 8, p. 97, July 15, p. 115, August 30, p. 235, September 27, p. 297, December 2, p. 486, December 30, 1921, p. 567, and January 27, 1922, pp. 79–80.

37. Interviews with Seymour Williams, June 2, 1978, Tulsa, W. D. Williams, June 7, 1978, Tulsa, Robert Fairchild, June 8, 1978, Tulsa, and V. H. Hodge, June 12, 1978, Tulsa; Henry Whitlow, "The History of the Greenwood Era in Tulsa," a paper presented to the Tulsa County Historical Society, March 29, 1973, p. 5. See also Tulsa *World*, June 15, 1921, p. 15; and Tulsa *Tribune*, June 2, 1921, p. 5.

38. Tulsa *World*, June 4, p. 18, June 6, p. 9, June 12, pp. A4, A12, June 16, p. 9, June 24, p. 1, and June 27, 1921, pp. 1, 10; Gill, "The Tulsa Race Riot," 74–75.

39. Interview with W. D. Williams, June 7, 1978, Tulsa; Record of Commission Proceedings, City of Tulsa, September 6, p. 248, September 9, p. 251, September 13, p. 261, September 16, pp. 275–76, September 27, p. 301, and October 7, 1921, p. 338; Tulsa *World*, June 10, p. 3, June 16, p. 9, June 24, pp. 1, 3, July 8, p. 9, July 15, p. 3, July 20, p. 18, July 26, p. 3, August 6, p. 16, and August 12, 1921, p. 2; Gill, "The Tulsa Race Riot," 73–77.

40. White to Preus, October 25, 1921, in Oklahoma State Attorney Generals Collection, Oklahoma State Archives.

41. Tulsa *World*, June 24, 1921, p. 9; Gill, "The Tulsa Race Riot," 83–85.

42. Interviews with W. D. Williams, June 7, 1978, Tulsa, and Robert Fairchild, June 8, 1978, Tulsa; Gill, "The Tulsa Race Riot," 83–85.

43. Tulsa *World*, June 2, 1921, p. 4.

44. Tulsa *Tribune*, June 2, p. 11, June 3, p. 20, June 4, p. 7, June 5, p. B10, June 6, p. 12, and June 7, 1921, p. 16; "The Tulsa Race Riots," *Independent*, CV (June 18, 1921), 647; Minutes of Directors' Meetings, Tulsa Chamber of Commerce, July 2, 1921, pp. 146–47.

45. Record of Commission Proceedings, City of Tulsa, July 8, p. 97, July 12, p. 110, August 2, p. 160, August 5, p. 165, August 9, p. 168, August 12, p. 173, August 26,

p. 223, September 30, p. 310, October 11, p. 351, October 14, p. 360, October 21, p. 375, December 2, p. 486, December 6, p. 501, December 16, p. 527, December 30, 1921, p. 567, and January 24, 1922, p. 70; interviews with W. D. Williams, June 7, 1978, Tulsa, and Robert Fairchild, June 8, 1978, Tulsa; Tulsa *World*, June 2, 1921, p. 1; Tulsa *Tribune*, June 3, p. 8, June 8, p. 2, June 9, pp. 1, 4, June 10, p. 9; June 11, p. 2, and June 14, 1921, p. 8; "Race Riot Quickens Public Conscience," *Harlow's Weekly*, XX (June 10, 1921), 47; "Mob Fury and Race Hatred as a National Danger," *Literary Digest*, LXIX (June 18, 1921), 7–9.

46. Tulsa *World*, July 21, p. 2, and December 24, 1921, p. 9; Parrish, *Events of the Tulsa Disaster*, 19–20; Gill, "The Tulsa Race Riot," 80–83.

47. Interview with W. D. Williams, June 7, 1978, Tulsa; Whitlow, "The History of the Greenwood Era in Tulsa," p. 5.

48. J. B. A. Robertson to S. P. Freeling, June 3, 1921, Civil Case 1062, Oklahoma State Attorney Generals Collection, Oklahoma State Archives; Tulsa *World*, June 3, pp. 1, 2, 8, June 5, p. A13, June 9, p. 16, June 10, p. 1, and June 24, 1921, p. 1; Tulsa *Tribune*, June 2, p. 1, June 3, p. 1, June 5, p. 1, June 7, p. 1, and June 8, 1921, p. 1.

49. Tulsa *World*, June 8, pp. 8, 18, June 9, p. 16, June 10, pp. 1, 8, June 11, p. 3, June 14, p. 13, June 16, p. 16, June 17, p. 1, June 19, p. 2, June 24, p. 1, and June 25, 1921, p. 1; Records for District Court Cases Nos. 2227, 2236, 2238–59, 2263, and 2265–66, in the Office of the Court Clerk, Tulsa County Courthouse, Tulsa.

50. Tulsa *World*, June 26, 1921, pp. 1, 8. Six months before the race riot, an editorial in the Tulsa *Star* dealt with the "issue" of "social equality." In part, the *Star* stated: "We are not demanding 'social equality'—that's something that regulates itself between individuals—but we are demanding all that any citizen of our country has a right to demand—Equality without discrimination" (November 27, 1920, p. 8).

51. Tulsa *World*, June 26, 1921, p. 8.

52. *Ibid.*

53. *Ibid.* This report was also published in the Tulsa *Tribune*, June 25, 1921, p. 1. Unfortunately, neither the original copy of the report, nor any materials associated with the grand jury could be located.

54. Victor E. Harlow, "Let Action Conform to Words," *Harlow's Weekly*, July 1, 1921, p. 1.

55. Records for District Court Cases Nos. 2227, 2236, 2238–2259, 2263, and 2265–2266, in the Office of the Court Clerk, Tulsa County Courthouse, Tulsa. Some black Tulsans, including hotel proprietor J. B. Stratford, fled the state, most likely to avoid possible arrest. Tulsa *Tribune*, June 16, p. 1, and June 20, 1921, p. 5; Gill, "The Tulsa Race Riot," 95–97; James E. Markham to S. P. Freeling, October 31, 1921, and, S. P. Freeling to James E. Markham, November 2, 1921, in Civil Case 1062, Oklahoma State Attorney Generals Collection, Oklahoma State Archives.

56. Records for District Court Cases Nos. 2227, 2236, 2238–2259, 2263, and 2265–2266, Office of the Court Clerk, Tulsa County Courthouse.

57. Gill, citing interviews he performed, believed that the Gustafson case might have been politically influenced by the dispute over the future water supply for Tulsa which was then in progress, and which, of course, involved the current city administration. He stated that "many were of the opinion that the purpose of the trial was to embarrass the city administration." Gill, "The Tulsa Race Riot," 100.

The Tulsa *Tribune* reported on June 18, 1921 that one "Garfield Thompson," black, had been convicted of carrying a concealed weapon during the riot, and was to serve thirty days in the county jail (p. 10). The author could not locate a person by that name among those indicted in the cases initiated by the grand jury (one Oscar Thompson, however, was located), and if such a person was convicted and sentenced, it may have been outside of the District Court. Tulsa *World*, June 11, 1921, p. 3.

One other case which concerned the riot was initiated in May, 1923, that of *William Redfearn, Plaintiff*, v. *the City of Tulsa, et al.*, which named the principal 1921 city and county government officials, plus three insurance companies, as defendants. The case was brought for loss and damages totaling $85,618.85, plus interest at 10 percent per annum. It was dismissed on February 11, 1937, for failure to prosecute.

The initiation of the *Redfearn* case in 1923 was by no means, however, the last time the race riot was heard of in Tulsa's courtrooms. Dr. John Hope Franklin, son of attorney B. C. Franklin (who played a key role in the defeat of the city's fire ordinance in 1921), informed the author that as a young man in Tulsa he would often go with his father to the courthouse. More than once on these occasions, Dr. Franklin stated, did he hear of litigations involving persons who had died "on or around" May 31 or June 1, 1921.

58. Records for Court Case No. 2239, Office of the Court Clerk, Tulsa County Courthouse.

## Chapter 5: The Segregation of Memory

1. In the early 1920s, Klansmen in Tulsa included the city's postmaster and, for a short time, the publisher of the Tulsa *Tribune*. There is also evidence to suggest that many white police officers belonged to the Klan. Charles C. Alexander, *The Ku Klux Klan in the Southwest* (Lexington: University of Kentucky Press, 1965), 265; Kenneth T. Jackson, *The Ku Klux Klan in the City* (New York: Oxford University Press, 1967), 239; interview with I. S. Pittman, July 28, 1978, Tulsa.

2. San Francisco *Chronicle*, June 4, 1921, p. 3; interviews with Seymour Williams, June 2, 1978, Tulsa, W. D. Williams, June 7, 1978, Tulsa, Robert Fairchild, June 8, 1978, Tulsa, and V. H. Hodge, June 12, 1978, Tulsa.

3. Alexander, *The Ku Klux Klan in the Southwest*, 98, 108, and 216. Arrell M. Gibson stated that the nationwide recession of 1921 "developed into a full-blown depression in Oklahoma," *Oklahoma: A History of Five Centuries* (Norman: Harlow Publishing Company, 1965), 358. Oklahoma's economy at that time was geared toward petroleum, cotton, and wheat, and each of these commodities took serious price falls from 1920 to 1921. In 1920, the average wholesale price of wheat was about $2.50 per bushel; in 1921, $1.33. A pound of raw cotton on the wholesale market averaged about $.34 in 1920; one year later, the average was only slightly above $.15 per pound. In 1920 and 1921, the average wholesale prices for a barrel of crude oil nationwide were, respectively, $3.07 and $1.73. The drop in price of crude oil in Oklahoma was even more dramatic. The price per barrel of 36-degrees Mid-Continent crude was around $3.50 in December 1920; eight months later, it was about $1.00 per barrel. These price falls led to some production stoppages, unemployment, and migration of the unemployed to the state's cities, including Tulsa. *Harlow's Weekly*, December 17, 1920, p. 6, and September

16, 1921, pp. 8, 13; Ralph Cassady, Jr., *Price Making and Price Behavior in the Petroleum Industry* (New Haven: Yale University Press, 1954), 136; United States Bureau of the Census, *Historical Statistics of the United States, Colonial Times to 1970* (Washington: Government Printing Office, 1975), II, 208; Record of Commission Proceedings, City of Tulsa, August 26, 1921, p. 220; and January 20, 1922, p. 55.

4. "Federal Vice Report on Vice Conditions in Tulsa," by Agent T. G. F., April 22–26, 1921, Civil Case 1062, Oklahoma State Attorney Generals Collection, Oklahoma State Archives.

5. *Ibid*; Tulsa *Star*, November 20, 1920, p. 8; Amy Comstock, "'Over There,' Another View of the Tulsa Riots," *Survey*, XLVI (July 2, 1921), 406; interview with W. D. Williams, June 7, 1978, Tulsa. See also James M. Mitchell, "Politics in a Boom Town: Tulsa From 1906 to 1930" (M.A. thesis, University of Tulsa, 1950), 31–33, 85–86, and "Local Findings on Record of Jno. A. Gustafson," Civil Case 1062, Oklahoma State Attorney Generals Collection, Oklahoma State Archives.

6. The harassment of black citizens by white police officers was not confined to black Tulsa; A. J. Smitherman reported that white officers threatened him downtown. Tulsa *Star*, September 4, p. 2, October 23, p. 1, November 20, 1920, p. 8, January 1, pp. 1, 8, and January 15, 1921, p. 2.

7. Kuznets and Thomas, *Population Redistribution and Economic Growth*, I, 576; United States Bureau of the Census, *Negroes in the United States, 1920–1932* (Washington: Government Printing Office, 1935), 793.

8. See Chapter 2.

9. Tulsa *Tribune*, May 31, 1921, in Loren L. Gill, "The Tulsa Race Riot" (M.A. thesis, University of Tulsa, 1946), p. 22 (italics added).

10. Alexander, *The Ku Klux Klan in the Southwest*, 66, 142–58, 228; David M. Chalmers, *Hooded Americanism: The History of the Ku Klux Klan* (Chicago: Quadrangle Books, 1965), 52–55; "K.K.K. Again," *New Statesman*, XXXII (1923), 135; Bruce Bliven, "From the Oklahoma Front," *New Republic* (October 17, 1923), 202.

11. Mary E. Jones Parrish, *Events of the Tulsa Disaster* (n.p., n.p., n.d.), 21–23.

12. Application for Charter of Tulsa, Oklahoma Branch of the National Association for the Advancement of Colored People, November 27, 1922; NAACP Director of Branches to Ernest Richards, Esq., September 11, 1926; NAACP Director of Branches to W. H. Williamson, June 25, 1930; all in Tulsa Branch Files, Box G-175, NAACP Papers, Library of Congress.

No further information was located regarding the Tulsa chapter of the African Blood Brotherhood. Although the national organization at first hedged the question as to whether its members were involved in the riot (probably because its New York office had not been contacted yet by Tulsa ABB members), it later openly associated itself with the steadfast self-defense shown by black Tulsans in the spring of 1921. The organization's initial statement, made by Cyril Briggs in New York City on June 5, 1921, read in part: "An article in the [New York] *Times* of June 4 implies responsibility on the part of the African Blood Brotherhood for the unfortunate bloody occurances [*sic*] in Tulsa, Okla. This organization has no other answer to make save admit that the African Blood Brotherhood is interested in having negroes organized for self-defense against wanton attack by whites," quoted in the New York *Times*, June 5, 1921, p. 21. The November, 1921, edition of the ABB's magazine, the *Crusader*, however, stated: "As We Have Done by You—Do You by Us! Remember *Tulsa*! Remember the Bright, Untarnished Record of the ABB! What Other Organization Can Match That Brave Record?", quoted in Theodore G. Vincent, *Black Power and the Garvey Movement* (San Francisco: Ramparts Press, 1972), 75.

13. See especially the excellent photographs in Ed Wheeler, "Profile of a Race Riot," *Oklahoma Impact Magazine*, IV (June–July, 1971), 16–27. Parrish, *Events of the Tulsa Disaster*, 23; *Tulsa City Directory, 1921* (Tulsa: Polk-Hoffhine Directory Co., 1921); Tulsa *World*, June 2, 1921, pp. 1–2. A copy of what was later reported as the official dead and wounded list is located in the Office of the Chief, Tulsa Police Department, Tulsa.

14. Connie Cronley, "That Ugly Day in May," *Oklahoma Monthly*, II (August, 1976), 33. The word *generous* is at issue here. As was shown in Chapter 4, white Tulsans did make *some* donations for relief work after the riot, perhaps totaling upward of $25,000. But as losses incurred due to the riot ran into the millions of dollars, the adjective "generous" is fallacious, especially considering the fabulous wealth that was present in some parts of the white community at that time.

15. Ralph Ellison, "The Golden Age/Time Past," *Esquire*, LI (January, 1959), 107.

16. "*Impact* Raps with W. D. Williams," *Oklahoma Impact*, IV (June–July, 1971), 36; Curlee Hackman, "Peg Leg Taylor and the Tulsa Race Riot," in J. M. Brewer (ed.), *American Negro Folklore* (Chicago: Quadrangle Books, 1968), 34–36; interview with W. D. Williams, June 7, 1978, Tulsa.

17. Tulsa *Tribune*, June 2, 1971, p. A7.

18. David Fritze, "The Fight Without a Finish," *Oklahoma Monthly*, IV (March, 1978), 32–60.

19. Ralph Ellison, "Remembering Jimmy," in *Shadow and Act* (New York: Random House, 1964), 242.

## EPILOGUE Notes on the Subsequent History of "Deep Greenwood"

1. Whitlow, "The History of the Greenwood Era in Tulsa," a paper presented to the Tulsa County Historical Society, March 29, 1973, p. 3.

2. *Ibid.*, 5–6.

3. *Ibid.*, 6.

4. Pat Cremin, "Greenwood is Fading," *Oklahoma Impact*, IV (June–July, 1971), 4–5.

# ESSAY ON SOURCES

Researching the history of the Tulsa race riot over a period of five years proved to be an experience that was both exhilarating and frustrating. More time than I care to think about was spent trying to track down sources which proved to be nonexistent. Other sources, particularly human ones, simply awaited someone to take an interest. In my quest for oral and written information, doors were both opened and closed, depending on mixtures of trust and mistrust or curiosity and apathy—yet another aspect of the vibrant legacy of the riot in Tulsa.

The following is intended to serve as a guide to the most important sources utilized in the book, and to direct interested readers to sources that were found to be particularly illuminating. Scholars in search of complete citations are directed to the notes and to the author's "The Tulsa Race Riot of 1921" (B.A. thesis, Reed College, 1976).

### KEY SOURCES

Three types of source material were critical to this book, and were heavily relied upon for information. The first of these were Tulsa newspapers. They proved to be essential in reconstructing the history of the IWW, Leonard, and Belton incidents, the race riot, and its aftermath. Eight of the period were used: the Oklahoma *Sun* (1921); the Tulsa *Democrat* (1917, 1919); the Tulsa *Guide* (1906); the Tulsa

*Star* (1914–1921); the Tulsa *Times* (1917–1919); the Tulsa *Tribune* (1920–1921); the Tulsa *Weekly Planet* (1912); and the Tulsa *World* (1917, 1919–1921). Of the white newspapers—the *Democrat*, the *Times*, the *Tribune*, and the *World*—the latter two proved to be the most useful. The city's black newspapers—*the Sun*, the *Guide*, the *Star*, and the *Weekly Planet*—were all helpful, but unfortunately, the extant issues of them are very few, and very far between. By far the most treasured issues were those of the *Star*. The Oklahoma *Eagle*, which has served as Tulsa's black newspaper for several decades, also contained useful information, particularly a series of articles on early Tulsa that ran in 1968.

My oral sources were absolutely essential. They provided balance for the often biased written materials and filled in the gaps where no materials existed. They were particularly useful in reconstructing the early history of black Tulsa (as many of the written materials pertaining to that history were consumed in the fires of the riot), and in describing the events of the riot and its aftermath. Nine of these remarkable individuals, all Tulsans, consented to taped interviews: B. E. Caruthers; V. H. Hodge; Robert Fairchild; Mrs. Mozella Jones; I. S. Pittman; Henry Whitlow; N. C. Williams; Seymour Williams; and W. D. Williams (the latter three are not related). Six of these individuals are black; three are white. At the time of the riot, their "occupations" included that of high school student, teacher, policeman, and laborer. The tapes of these interviews (two complete sets) have been deposited in two locations: the McFarlin Library at the University of Tulsa; and the Manuscript Division of the Perkins Library at Duke University.

The third critical type of source materials was certain collections of public and private records. Although the National Association for the Advancement of Colored People Papers at the Library of Congress and the Socialist Party of America Papers at Duke University proved to be helpful, by far the most important collections were those in Oklahoma. The Governor James B. A. Robertson Papers and the Oklahoma State Attorney Generals Collection, both located in the Oklahoma State Archives in Oklahoma City, contained valuable information on the riot and its aftermath, as did, to a lesser extent, the Redmond S. Cole Papers in the Western Historical Collection at the University of Oklahoma. More important, however, were: the Record of Commission Proceedings (1921–1922) of the City of Tulsa, located at the Office of the Commission Secretary, City Hall, Tulsa; the Court Records in the Office of the Court Clerk, Tulsa County Courthouse, Tulsa; and, the Minutes of the Directors' Meetings of the Chamber of Commerce, located in the offices of the Metropolitan Tulsa Chamber of Commerce, Tulsa.

### TULSA HISTORY

We do not possess a good, scholarly history of Tulsa, nor has the city been the subject of many articles in historical journals—a sad neglect of the richness of the city's past. Angie Debo, *Tulsa: From Creek Town to Oil Capital* (Norman: University of Oklahoma Press, 1943), is a brief history which attempts to place the city's development into a broad perspective. A better, though "nonscholarly," work is William Butler, *Tulsa 75: A History of Tulsa* (Tulsa: Metropolitan Tulsa Chamber of Commerce, 1974), which is filled with a large amount of useful information. James Monroe Hall, *The Beginning of Tulsa* (Tulsa: Scott-Rice Company, 1928), and Clarence B. Douglas, *The History of Tulsa, Oklahoma: A City with a Personality*, (3 vols.; Chicago: S. J. Clarke Publishing Company, 1921), are primarily useful as source material.

Unfortunately, none of these authors—with the possible exception of Butler—was particularly interested in charting the history of black Tulsa. Fortunately, a number of my interviewees were, and they were heavily relied upon. One of them, Henry Whitlow, also provided me with a copy of his excellent "A History of the Greenwood Era in Tulsa," a paper presented to the Tulsa County Historical Society, March 29, 1973. This is a succinct social history of the Greenwood business district. Extant copies of black Tulsa newspapers also proved useful.

A wealth of information on vice conditions in Tulsa is located in the Oklahoma State Attorney Generals Collection and the Governor James B. A. Robertson Papers, both located in the Oklahoma State Archives. Unfortunately, no records of the Tulsa police department prior to the 1940s exist.

A good source on the early political life of Tulsa is James M.

Mitchell, "Politics in a Boom Town: Tulsa From 1906 to 1930" (M.A. thesis, University of Tulsa, 1950). Articles from *Harlow's Weekly*, an Oklahoma news magazine, and the *Tulsa Spirit*, the journal of the Tulsa Chamber of Commerce, and material from *Tulsa City Directories* proved to be helpful in charting the economic history of the city.

WORLD WAR I ERA RACE RELATIONS

A wealth of material has been published in the past two decades on the history of race riots and racial violence in America. A good place to start is Chapter 7 ("Living Together Violently: Blacks and Whites in America from the Colonial Period to 1970") in Richard Maxwell Brown, *Strain of Violence: Historical Studies of American Violence and Vigilantism* (New York: Oxford University Press, 1975). Of the several studies of World War I era race riots, by far the most helpful was William M. Tuttle, Jr., *Race Riot: Chicago in the Red Summer of 1919* (New York: Atheneum, 1972). On lynching, the most useful sources were: the National Association for the Advancement of Colored People (NAACP) Papers, Library of Congress; NAACP, *Thirty Years of Lynching in the United States, 1889–1918*, plus supplements (New York: NAACP, 1919–1921); and, Monroe N. Work (ed.), *Negro Year Book: An Annual Encyclopedia of the Negro, 1925–1926* (Tuskegee Institute, Alabama: Negro Year Book Publishing Company, 1925).

I. A. Newby, *Jim Crow's Defense: Anti-Negro Thought in America, 1900–1930* (Baton Rouge: Louisiana State University Press, 1965), and John Higham, *Strangers in the Land: Patterns of American Nativism, 1860–1925* (New York: Atheneum, 1963), proved to be the most helpful general works on the particularly violent manifestations of white racism during the period. On the Ku Klux Klan, by far the most useful book for this study was Charles C. Alexander, *The Ku Klux Klan in the Southwest* (Lexington: University of Kentucky Press, 1965). Other useful items on the Klan, both nationally and in Oklahoma, include: David M. Chalmers, *Hooded Americanism: The History of the Ku Klux Klan* (Chicago: Quadrangle Books, 1965); Kenneth T. Jackson, *The Ku Klux Klan in the City, 1915–1930* (New York: Oxford University Press, 1967); and, Marion

Monteval, *The Klan Inside Out* (Claremore, Oklahoma: Monarch Publishing Company, 1924).

On trends of black thought in the United States during this period, a good place to start is John Hope Franklin, *From Slavery to Freedom: A History of Negro Americans* (4th ed.; New York: Alfred A. Knopf, 1974). There are a number of other extremely useful books. One illuminating, but apparently little used, volume is Robert T. Kerlin, *The Voice of the Negro, 1919* (1920; rpt. New York: Arno Press and the New York Times, 1968). One should also consult two excellent books by Theodore G. Vincent: *Black Power and the Garvey Movement* (San Francisco: Ramparts Press, 1972); and *Voices of a Black Nation: Political Journalism of the Harlem Renaissance* (San Francisco: Ramparts Press, 1973). Each contain information on the African Blood Brotherhood.

Black history and the history of race relations in Oklahoma have not received the attention they warrant. By far the most useful general work is Kay M. Teall (ed.), *Black History in Oklahoma: A Resource Book* (Oklahoma City: Oklahoma City Public Schools, 1971). Teall's volume is an enticing compilation of source material on black Oklahoma history from the 1500s to the 1970s. Other items which proved to be of assistance were: Arthur Tolson, *The Black Oklahomans: A History, 1541–1972* (New Orleans: Edwards Printing Company, 1972), a general survey; Edwin S. Redkey, *Black Exodus: Black Nationalism and Back-to-Africa Movements, 1890–1910* (New Haven: Yale University Press, 1969), which discusses Chief Alfred Sam; and, Norman L. Crockett, *The Black Towns* (Lawrence: Regents Press of Kansas, 1979), and William Bittle and Gilbert L. Geis, "Racial Self-Fulfillment and the Rise of an All-Negro Community in Oklahoma," in August Meier and Elliott Rudwick (eds.), *The Making of Black America*, II (New York: Atheneum, 1969).

### OKLAHOMA RADICALISM AND THE IWW INCIDENT

The history of political radicalism in the Sooner State has fared better. Two recent works are: James M. Green, *Grass-Roots Socialism: Radical Movements in the Southwest, 1885–1943* (Baton Rouge: Louisiana State University Press, 1978); and, Garin Burbank, *When*

*Farmers Voted Red: The Gospel of Socialism in the Oklahoma Countryside, 1910–1914* (Westport, Conn.: Greenwood Press, 1976). Green's book is by far the stronger of the two, and is filled with a tremendous amount of valuable information. David A. Shannon, *The Socialist Party of America: A History* (Chicago: Quadrangle Books, 1955), and James A. Weinstein, *The Decline of Socialism in America, 1912–1921* (New York: Monthly Review Press, 1967), were helpful in fathoming the history of the socialist movement in Oklahoma, as were the Oklahoma state files of the Socialist Party of America Papers at Duke University. The most useful general history of the IWW was Melvyn Dubofsky, *We Shall Be All: A History of the Industrial Workers of the World* (Chicago: Quadrangle Books, 1969).

The primary sources for the IWW incident in Tulsa were three (white) Tulsa newspapers—the *Times*, the *World*, and the *Democrat*—plus, National Civil Liberties Bureau, *The "Knights of Liberty" Mob and the I.W.W. Prisoners at Tulsa, Okla., November 9, 1917* (New York: National Civil Liberties Bureau, 1918), a pamphlet containing the results of their investigation. Information about the incident is also to be found in: William T. Lampe, *Tulsa County and the World War* (Tulsa: Tulsa County Historical Society, 1918), which eulogizes the Knights of Liberty; H. C. Peterson and Gilbert Fite, *Opponents of War, 1917–1918* (Seattle: University of Washington Press, 1957), an excellent history of both the antiwar movement and radical suppression in America; and Joyce L. Kornbluh (ed.), *Rebel Voices: An I.W.W. Anthology* (Ann Arbor: University of Michigan Press, 1964). Kornbluh's excellent volume also contains some information on the Oil Field Workers Union, as does Federal Writers' Project of Oklahoma, *Labor History of Oklahoma* (Oklahoma City: A. M. Van Horn, 1939). No extant issues of black Tulsa newspapers contained any information relating to this incident.

### LEONARD AND BELTON INCIDENTS

My information on the events surrounding the fatal shooting of O. W. Leonard is based almost entirely on accounts in three white Tulsa newspapers: the *Times*, the *World*, and the *Democrat*. Unfortunately, once again, no copies of what was then the city's black newspaper, the *Star*, seemed to have survived with information on the incident. With the exception of W. D. Williams, who provided some inferential information, none of my oral informants could provide me with any information on the incident.

The account of the lynching of Roy Belton was derived from a similar data base. Although the event is mentioned in Walter White, "The Eruption of Tulsa" *Nation*, CXII (June, 1921), my primary sources were the accounts of the *World* and the *Tribune*. A small amount of information, mainly important for its editorial content, was found in a rare issue of the *Star*. A collection of brief newspaper clippings about the incident is located in the NAACP Papers at the Library of Congress.

### THE RACE RIOT

Although this book has differed significantly in both its sources of information and its interpretation, it has nonetheless benefited from prior studies of the riot. Additionally, the two earliest studies proved to be particularly helpful as the sources of material no longer in existence.

It is truly unfortunate that so little could be discovered about Mary E. Jones Parrish, for her *Events of the Tulsa Disaster* (N.p., n.p., n.d.), the first book about the riot, is in many ways a truly remarkable document. My oral informants felt that she had come to Tulsa, where she worked as a teacher, only shortly before the riot, and departed soon afterwards. *Events of the Tulsa Disaster* is a difficult book to classify. It is both a finely detailed personal memoir of her experiences during the riot as well as compilation of statements of other riot victims about the event. She also included some statistical information regarding riot losses. Yet, regardless how one types this work, it is an important source for the history of the riot.

Loren L. Gill's "The Tulsa Race Riot" (M.A. thesis, University of Tulsa, 1946) was the first "historical" study of the riot. It not only charts the events of the violence and its aftermath, but attempts to place the riot within the broader contexts of both Tulsa and American history. Gill was a dogged researcher, and his thesis remains as a crucial source on the contents of the May 31, 1921, issue of the Tulsa *Tribune*. Gill also performed oral interviews with a number of since-deceased Tulsans about the riot and its aftermath and, since the notes to these interviews have been lost, his thesis remains the only source of their contents. While well-researched, "The Tulsa Race Riot" suffers in its interpretive abilities due in no small part to a patronizing attitude toward blacks. (It bears notation, however, that shortly before his untimely death in the early 1970s, Gill informed his thesis adviser that his feelings about the riot had changed considerably over the years.) His interpretation of the aftermath of the riot suffers from portraying the actions of the city's white elite in a better light than they deserve (which may have been due, in part, to lack of access to certain materials), and, like the other studies, he did not recognize the importance of the IWW and Leonard incidents in the creation of a local atmosphere which would allow the riot to occur.

Subsequent studies of the riot have been less energetically researched than Loren Gill's thesis. Lee E. Williams and Lee E. Williams II, *Anatomy of Four Race Riots: Racial Conflict in Knoxville, Elaine (Arkansas), Tulsa and Chicago, 1919–1921* (Hattiesburg: University and College Press of Mississippi, 1972), contains a balanced chapter on the riot based primarily on national magazine articles. R. Halliburton, Jr., *The Tulsa Race War of 1921* (San Francisco: R and E Research Associates, 1975), is primarily a collection of documents about the riot. Halliburton's narrative text, which closely follows his "The Tulsa Race War of 1921," *Journal of Black Studies*, XX (March, 1972), suffers primarily from its brevity. Halliburton is to be credited, however, for being the first to utilize certain previously ignored sources of information about the riot. Of the popular magazine articles about the riot, the most helpful was Ed Wheeler, "Profile of a Race Riot," *Oklahoma Impact Magazine*, IV (June–July, 1971).

The Tulsa race riot was "national news" and was the subject of a fair number of articles in national periodicals. "The Tulsa Race Riots," *Independent*, CV (June 18, 1921); "Blood and Oil," *Survey*, XLVI (June 11, 1921); "The Lesson of Tulsa," *Outlook*, CXXVIII (June 15, 1921); and "The Tulsa Riots," *Crisis*, XXII (July 1921), all contain useful information, but the most useful is Walter White, "The Eruption of Tulsa," *Nation*, CXII (June 29, 1921). White, who at that time served on the national staff of the NAACP, traveled to Tulsa incognito to investigate the devastation. Amy Comstock, "'Over There,'

Another View of the Tulsa Riots," *Survey*, XLVI (July 2, 1921), is an attempt to relieve white Tulsans for any responsibility in the event, written by the secretary to Richard Lloyd Jones, editor of the *Tribune*.

Charles F. Barrett, *Oklahoma after Fifty Years: A History of the Sooner State and Its People* (Hopkinsville, Ky.: Historical Record Association, 1941), vacillates between being a personal memoir and a history of the state. Barrett was the adjutant general of Oklahoma at the time of the riot, commanding the National Guard troops which came to the city. His section on the riot contains a good amount of useful information. A reminiscence of value is Ross T. Warner, *Oklahoma Boy* (N.p., n.p., n.d.).

Newspaper accounts were essential in reconstructing the events of the riot. Not surprisingly, the material found in the *Tribune* and the *World* was found to be the most helpful. The offices of the *Star* and the *Sun* were burned by white rioters, and the nearest extant issues of each do not contain any information especially helpful in charting the course of the violence. Of the out-of-town newspapers consulted, those found to be of the most assistance were: the New York *Times*; the San Francisco *Chronicle*; the Oklahoma City *Daily Oklahoman*; and the Oklahoma City *Black Dispatch*.

In the face of this situation—the dearth of local black sources— the testimony of many of my oral informants proved to be particularly valuable. Not only did they balance the accounts in the *Tribune* and the *World*, but they also provided information on personal experiences during the violence simply not available anywhere else.

The collections of the Oklahoma State Archives also proved to be invaluable in charting the course of the violence. The Governor James B. A. Robertson Papers contain a number of important documents, including the telegrams sent him by the authorities in Tulsa. The Oklahoma State Attorney Generals Collection also contains a number of key items, including statements by Tulsans affected by the riot.

THE AFTERMATH

The events comprising the aftermath of the riot were also reconstructed from an amalgam of sources. Testimony from my oral infor-

mants, plus accounts in the *Tribune* and the *World*, covered the entire range of post-riot activities. One extant issue of the *Sun* also
contained useful material.

In documenting the activities of the city's white elite, the key
sources were the Records of Commission Proceedings (1921–1922),
City of Tulsa, and, especially, the Minutes of Directors' Meetings
(1921), Tulsa Chamber of Commerce. Other notably useful items on
this topic, and on the bona fide relief activities, included: Gill, "The
Tulsa Race Riot," which contains information culled from his interviews; Parrish, *Events of the Tulsa Disaster*, for her information on
the Red Cross and various black groups; and, White, "The Eruption
of Tulsa," for its knowledgeable perspective on what was actually
transpiring during the "reconstruction."

Barrett, *Oklahoma after Fifty Years*, the Robertson Papers at the
Oklahoma State Archives, and Douglas, *The History of Tulsa*, I,
were helpful in fathoming the involvement of the National Guard.
The records of the District Court Clerk, located in the Tulsa County
Courthouse were central to an understanding of the legal aspects of
the aftermath, as were materials in the Oklahoma State Attorney
Generals Collection at the Oklahoma State Archives.

### USE OF CITY DIRECTORIES

*Tulsa City Directories*, from 1909 to 1922, were used in a number of ways in the research of this book, from trying to gain a sense
who the IWW prisoners were to gauging the destruction of black
Tulsa during the riot. They were an important source for the map,
"Central Tulsa, 1917–1921," and were virtually the only source for
Appendices I and II. The research processes used with the directories
were elementary, though often time-consuming. They bear explana-
tion for their applicability to other research in urban social history,
particularly in those subjects where manuscript census data is either
not available or not particularly helpful.

Those familiar with city directories know that they share a number of things in common with a modern telephone directory, but
that they contain more information. The most complete directories
that I employed contained four sections: a general information section; an alphabetical index; an index of businesses; and a street in-

dex. The first section, the general information section, is a listing of public officials, public buildings, important commercial buildings, religious institutions, and fraternal orders. This section provided information on a number of subjects, including: how large the Tulsa police force was at any given year; how many police officers were black (in Tulsa city directories for this period, any person or institution designated as black was followed by a "(c)"—for "colored"); the location of important buildings; and the number, age, and congregation size of the city's black churches (Appendix I was taken completely from this section).

The bulk of the city directories is taken up by the second section, the alphabetical index. This section, which resembles the "white pages" of a telephone book, purports to be an alphabetical listing of all of the city's individuals and businesses. (One should assume that the completeness of such a compilation is as questionable as a manuscript census schedule—if not more so). An individual entry in this section might contain the following information: name of the (male) head of household; race, if black; spouse's name; occupation; employer or place of employment; and residence address. This section of the city directory was used, for example, to determine the race and occupations of the IWW defendants and the persons subpoenaed in the Robinson case.

The third section, the index of businesses, closely resembles the "yellow pages" of a telephone book. Headings for a particular type of business or business person were followed by a listing of: persons or firms engaged in that line of work; their race, if black; and their addresses. Appendix II is based upon a simple enumeration of all black business persons and establishments as they appeared in this section of extant Tulsa city directories from 1907 to 1923.

Most of the Tulsa city directories from this period also contain a fourth section: a street index. This is a listing of all of the streets in Tulsa, followed by a listing of what, or who, resided at each address. From this it is possible to get a precise picture of of the distribution of black and white sections of the city, as well as the layout of business and residential districts. We can learn even more about these blocks if we combine this information with that found in the alphabetical index. By looking up each resident in the 500 block of North

Detroit Avenue, in the 1921 directory, we discover, for example, that most of them were married. We also learn what their occupations were and, for these particular blocks, this information is quite revealing. The white male residents (for whom an occupation was listed) were primarily unskilled and skilled workers. Many of their black male neighbors, by contrast, were professionals. Indeed, the 500 block of North Detroit was the home of a large portion of the city's black elite, including two physicians, one dentist, one druggist, the editor of the *Star*, and the principal of the Booker T. Washington School.

Information from this section of the city directories was employed in a number of ways, but was particularly useful in mapping Tulsa's black community. By using this section, as in the above example, in conjunction with period maps and plat maps obtained from the City Engineer's office in Tulsa, I was able to designate the city's black and white neighborhoods in the map, "Central Tulsa, 1917–1921." This section was also helpful in investigating the social geography of the city and in trying to gauge the destruction of the riot.

# Acknowledgments

Had it not been for the help of three historians, this book most likely would not have been written. John Strawn, of Portland, Oregon, opened my eyes to the substance of the nation's past in his brilliantly constructed course on American social history, and patiently guided me through the first version of this work. In Tulsa, W. D. Williams graciously took me into his home on several occasions, openly shared his personal experiences, allowed treasured family artifacts to be photographed, and diligently led me through the history of our hometown. After forty-two years of public service in teaching at Booker T. Washington High School in Tulsa, in 1979 the State of Oklahoma intelligently bestowed upon Mr. Williams the honorary title of "Historian of Oklahoma." Larry Goodwyn's help virtually defies description. As my mentor in the Oral History Program at Duke University, he encouraged me to continue my work on the riot, looked the other way when it interfered with my dissertation, and offered keen insights and crucial advice and criticism along the way.

Other historians have also been of assistance. The early and sustained encouragement of Bill Tuttle of the University of Kansas has been especially gratifying. The same may be said of Bill Chafe of the Oral History Program at Duke, who also assisted in securing funds for my research. Other scholars generously read and criticized various drafts of this work. They are: William McClendon of the Port-

151

land *Observer* in Portland, Oregon; Raymond Gavins of Duke University; Peter Decker of the Double D Ranch, Ridgway, Colorado; William Strickland of the University of Massachusetts; Patrick Blessing and William Settle of the University of Tulsa; and Henry Whitlow, former principal of Booker T. Washington High School, Tulsa. Mr. Whitlow's and Mr. Settle's insights into the history of Tulsa proved to be essential, and they and Mr. Blessing did much to help facilitate my research in Oklahoma.

The Duke Oral History Program also deserves recognition. Although my earliest work on the riot preceded my affiliation with Duke, this book has been substantially affected by the program's rigorous methods and democratic philosophy in the investigation of American history. In particular, two of my fellow graduate students at Duke, Donna Benson and Randy Lawrence, have significantly shaped and added to my understanding of the American past and have offered what is perhaps the best advice of all: that of one's peers.

The indispensable contributions of my oral informants should be obvious. W. D. Williams, Henry Whitlow, Robert Fairchild, N. C. Williams, and the late Seymour Williams deserve special recognition, not only for their time and patience, but also for leading me to other informants. Mrs. Mozella Jones aided me in a similar fashion, and also arranged for me to meet her brother, Dr. John Hope Franklin, whose encouragement has been notably gratifying.

In my search for written information, I was ably assisted by the staffs of a number of institutions. I would especially like to give thanks to the staffs of the following: the Tulsa City-County Library, Central Branch; the McFarlin Library of the University of Tulsa (especially Dr. Guy Logsdon); the Oklahoma State Historical Society (with a special thanks to Mrs. Mary Moran, who ably manages the newspaper archive); the Tulsa County Historical Society (particularly Mrs. Ruth Avery, another scholar of the riot); the Publications and Communications Office of the Metropolitan Tulsa Chamber of Commerce; and three Tulsa newspapers, the Oklahoma *Eagle*, the Tulsa *Tribune*, and the Tulsa *World*.

This book has been shaped over the years by a number of individuals who also have provided needed support and encouragement. While most of them are involved in pursuits far afield from American social history, their questions about my work have shaped it significantly. Others assisted in ways ranging from housing me to helping me with the various drafts. In particular, I would like to thank Carolyn Billings, Elise Butler, John Fawley, Wade Hockett, Jeff Jacobs, George and Mary Sue McDaniel, Rachel Mason, Jim Pearson, Craig and Kathy Ryan, Roberta Stein, and Jane Vessels. At LSU Press, I have benefited from the interest and ideas of Marie Blanchard and Beverly Jarrett.

There is one other group which has significantly affected this book. Any author seeks a universal audience, but there are always a few, finite groups to whom a work is directed. One of mine is the Class of 1972 at Tulsa Central High School. As most of us were born in 1954, we were literally the children of the *Brown* decision, the children of integrated public schools. We were a true microcosm of the city of Tulsa, of all races and all social classes. Our three years together were marked by both large-scale racial violence and small-scale attempts at racial understanding. My classmates, many of them close friends, and our experiences together have very much remained in the back of my mind in the writing of this book. They have both fueled its creation and altered its form.

Lastly, I would like to thank my family. My brother generously lent me the use of his camera, and my sister provided me with important information about the musical history of Tulsa. My parents deserve the most credit of all. Throughout the process they have been a constant source of support. Indeed, they may have played a much larger role in the coming about of this book than they might imagine. When I was very young, my mother read me a history of the world, and my father taught me about rocks, fossils, and the geologic history of Oklahoma. I think this must have played a part.

# Index